AN EDUCATOR'S GUIDE
2ND EDITION
to living a virtuous life

Sister John Dominic Rasmussen, OP
and Dominican Sisters of Mary, Mother of the Eucharist

DISCIPLE of CHRIST
EDUCATION IN VIRTUE®

LUMEN ECCLESIAE PRESS

Copyright © 2018 Education in Virtue. All rights reserved. No part of this publication may be reproduced or transmitted in any form or means, electronic or mechanical, including photocopy, recording, or information storage and retrieval system, without the permission in writing from the publisher.

Published by Lumen Ecclesiae Press

    4101 East Joy Road

    Ann Arbor, Michigan 48105

Catechism of the Catholic Church quotes taken from the English translation of the *Catechism of the Catholic Church* for the United States of America copyright © 1994, United States Catholic Conference—Liberia Editrice Vaticana. English translation of the *Catechism of the Catholic Church*: Modifications from the Edito Typica copyright © 1997, United States Catholic Conference, Inc.—Liberia Editrice Vaticana.

Unless otherwise noted, all Scripture texts in this work are taken from the New American Bible, revised edition © 2010, 1991, 1986, 1970 Confraternity of Christian Doctrine, Washington, D.C. and are used by permission of the copyright owner. All rights reserved. No part of the New American Bible may be reproduced in any form without permission in writing from the copyright owner.

Cover Design: Amy Beers

Kerygma Tree: Sister Emmanuel Gross, OP

Virtue Tree Illustration: Sister Mary Grace Thul, OP

Book Design Layout: Gail Nicklowitz, Linda Kelly, Amy Beers

Contributors: Sister Jude Andrew Link, OP, Dominican Sisters of Mary, Mother of the Eucharist, Sally Wagner

Copy Editor: Claudia Volkman

Requests for permission to make copies of any part of the work should be directed to: info@educationinvirtue.com.

Nihl Obstat: Monsignor Robert Lunsford

                  Censor Librorium

Imprimatur: † Earl Boyea

                  Bishop of Lansing

                  May 21, 2018

Printed with Ecclesiastical Permission. Most Reverend Earl Boyea, Bishop of Lansing.

ISBN 978-0-9982607-7-8

Second Edition

Printed in the United States of America

*Dedicated to the students and alumni of
Spiritus Sanctus Academy*

May you always live as joyful disciples of Christ.

Foreword

The Catholic Church attaches great importance to the education of young people. Because the Church insists that we respect the truth about the good of the human person, moral instruction occupies a central place within Catholic pedagogy. What the Church requires Catholic educators to teach about the moral life, centers around the Ten Commandments. We find this instruction in the Third Part of the *Catechism of the Catholic Church*. It is one thing, however, to instruct about the truth, and it is another to teach how to live the truth. For instance, it is one thing to learn the Fifth Commandment, "You shall not kill;" another to know what to do when feelings of anger arise within the human heart. It is one thing to receive instruction in matters pertaining to sexual morality; another to discover the properly Catholic way to refrain from indulging movements of the soul that lead to acting unchastely. From the first centuries of the Christian era, holy men and women have taught about the Christian virtues as a way to practice holiness of life.

One finds great advantage in teaching children about the four cardinal virtues and their many auxiliary virtues. First of all, the virtues point the child toward various excellences of character that the human family traditionally has recognized as praiseworthy. What is more important, this program of instruction communicates to the child that he or she should not consider Catholic discipline something that places strict limits and heavy burdens on human freedom. As the many examples drawn from the lives of the saints demonstrate, the disciple of Christ inherits perfections, not limitations.

It pleases me greatly that Sister John Dominic Rasmussen, O.P., with the help of her religious community, the Dominican Sisters of Mary, Mother of the Eucharist, have produced course materials that aim to instruct young people in the Christian virtues. This course communicates the perfections of character that arise from living faithfully within the Catholic Church and in the company of her saints. It shows that the practice of the Christian virtues inculcates in the young Catholic an appreciation for the perfection of human freedom which the Church describes as happiness or blessedness.

Romanus Cessario, O.P.
Boston, 29, April 2018
Feast of Saint Catherine of Siena

TABLE OF CONTENTS

Introduction...6

Section 1 | Why Educate in Virtue?
Pages 7–14

The Good News...8

Living as a Disciple of Christ...12

Section 2 | What Are the Virtues?
Pages 15–129

The Road Map...16

Overview of the Virtues and Gifts...18

Theological Virtues
- Faith...23
- Hope...35
- Charity...49

Cardinal Virtues
- Prudence...59
- Justice...73
- Fortitude...97
- Temperance...111

Section 3 | Who Lives and Teaches Virtue?
Pages 131–139

Personal Application
- Living Virtuously...131
- Living as a Disciple of Christ...136

Section 4 | How to Educate in Virtue?
Pages 141–161

Creating a Culture of Virtue in Your School
- Virtue Chart...138
- Learn, Live Witness...142
- Living Virtuously is Discipline...144
- Resources...149
- Glossary...159

Introduction

This book is an aid for educators and parents in understanding the importance of living a virtuous life. Hence, it will assist you in teaching those entrusted to your care. Each section answers the following questions: why, what, who, and how to educate in virtue.

Why educate in virtue? Section one answers this question by providing a big picture of the key points of the kerygma, or first proclamation. These include God's loving plan for us, sin, and its consequences, God's answer—sending His Son, and our response.

Understanding "the why" from this perspective is fundamental to the purpose and meaning of living a virtuous life. It not only enables us to order our interior life, but it also gives shape to our view of life and the world. As disciples of Christ, we simply see the world and the events of the world differently. "The one who has hope lives differently" (Pope Benedict XVI *Spe Salvi*, 2). External situations may stay the same, but the Christian lives differently in the world because his eyes are "fixed on Jesus, the leader and perfecter" of his or her faith (Hebrews 12:2).

What are the virtues? Section two begins with a road map of what lies ahead in the following chapters. Each chapter covers a virtue from different angles—Know it; Guard it; Pray it; Live it; and Going Deeper. Each cardinal virtue has virtues that are allied or related. These are developed to provide a more thorough understanding of how the virtues are interconnected.

Who lives and teaches virtue? The why and what must be lived, taught, and modeled. This section speaks directly to us—"the who"—and goes deeper into the fourth part of the kerygma: our response to God's love. We are responsible for knowing, living, and witnessing to the Person of Jesus Christ. In order for our lives to bear fruit and to assist those entrusted to our care, our interior life must be integrated and rooted in Christ.

How to educate in virtue? Based on the theme of learn, live, and witness, section four answers the "how." It provides practical applications that will give direction for anyone interested in educating in virtue. The positive language of virtue changes the culture of a home, school, or workplace. It provides meaning to living a well-ordered and disciplined lifestyle. For we were created to live in harmony with God, creation, oneself, and others. Once this way of life is embraced, we become fully alive, for as St. Gregory of Nyssa taught—"The goal of the virtuous life is to become like God."

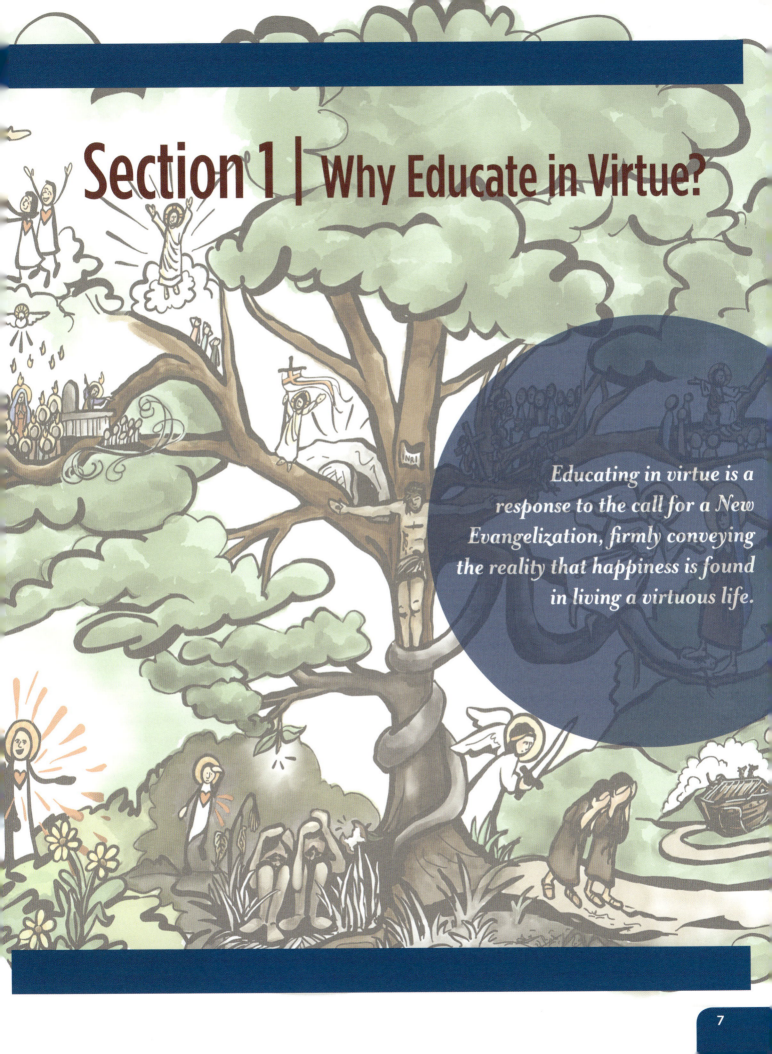

Section 1 | Why Educate in Virtue?

Educating in virtue is a response to the call for a New Evangelization, firmly conveying the reality that happiness is found in living a virtuous life.

The Good News

The purpose of this introduction is to provide you with the "big picture" in which you can fit this guide, and all the *Disciple of Christ—Education in Virtue* materials. The "big picture" is the kerygma.

Kerygma is a Greek word for "proclamation." The early apostles joyfully proclaimed all they had seen and heard firsthand from living and knowing Jesus Christ. As credible witnesses, their teachings "cut to the heart" (Acts 2:37) and lead many to conversion. The kerygma can be best understood by focusing on four key points: 1) God's loving plan; 2) sin and its consequences; 3) God sending His Son for our redemption; 4) our response of love. We, too, are called to be credible witnesses and to live joyfully as disciples of Christ.

> *"What we have seen and heard, we proclaim now to you, so that you too may have fellowship with us; for our fellowship is with the Father and with his Son, Jesus Christ."*
>
> *1 John 1:3*

Each one of us longs for happiness; each one of us desires wholeness. We long for meaning, to know the purpose and direction of our lives. Created in God's image and likeness, we have deep within us echoes of God's voice, echoes of the greatness for which we are destined. God made us to share in His own divine life, to find our fulfillment in Him. This is our hope, this is our purpose—to be with Him, finding our happiness in Him. **This is Good News.**

Created by Love, Called to Love

"God is love" (1 John 4:8). With this short, dynamic statement, John gives us an insight into who God is. In revealing Himself, God shares with us His "innermost secret: God Himself is an eternal exchange of love, Father, Son, and Holy Spirit, and He has destined us to share in that exchange" (*CCC*, 221). Love freely gives, desiring the good of the beloved, cherishing the uniqueness and dignity of the other. God is love, and everything He does is an outpouring of this love. He made us to share in this love, creating us in His own image and likeness thus setting us, raising us, higher than the rest of creation. He has bestowed upon us gifts of nature and grace. We have been given an intellect to know the good and a will to choose it. God has gifted us with freedom, for love would not be love if it were not freely given and received. We are able to hear the voice of our Father, to listen to Him and obey Him. John goes even further to reveal who we are as children of our heavenly Father. "God first loved us" (1 John 4:19)—this reality marks our relationship with Him. If we carefully listen, we will hear Him say to us, "I love you." To which we can only naturally reply by saying, "I love you too."

Hence, at the origin of creation, there was harmony and order; harmony with God, with self, with each other, and with all of creation. This is what is meant by original holiness and justice. There was a freedom and joy in their communion and friendship with God and their actions were oriented toward God and each other. Each day God came to walk with them in the Garden and this paradigm of His seeking us has never ceased.

Where Are You?

Tragically, the harmony and order was ruptured and spun into chaos. The serpent, "the most cunning of all the wild animals" (Genesis 3:1), had already made the choice to disobey God, choosing isolation and separation from God. This serpent came to our first parents and placed within Eve a seed of doubt. Is God good? Does He desire your happiness? Do you really need to obey His voice? Adam and Eve allowed their trust in the Creator to die in their hearts, and, abusing the freedom given them, chose to turn away from God (*CCC*, 397). Instead, they listened and followed the voice of the deceiver.

Immediately God comes to them, to walk with them. Instead of the free and easy self-communication of their earlier encounters, this one opens with the heartrending question, "Where are you?" Where, indeed, are they? They are far from themselves, frightened of God and of each other. The law of domination, use, and power has entered into the dynamics of human interactions. Within themselves, they experience the frustration and chaos of conflicting emotions and desires. The intellect is clouded by ignorance; the will is wrapped in weakness. Death's finality is the inescapable sign of what it means to live apart from God, apart from life. Instead of delighting in the beauty of the Garden, they now use it to hide from their Maker. "Where are you?" God asks. From their position of rupture, Adam and Eve struggle to listen to the voice of God. Instead of hearing the voice of a Father who loves them, they hear the voice of a powerful, perhaps vengeful, God, so they hide from Him. Their Father, however, assures them of His love and His mercy, by announcing His plan of salvation, the Protoevangelium, that the woman will crush the head of the serpent (Genesis 3:15).

Love Comes Down

God wants to be with us; He does not abandon us. He loves us. He loves us at every moment: His love is what sustains our very existence. He knows all our weaknesses and sins and still loves us. Desiring our wholeness and happiness, He calls us to repentance and communion with Him. The temptation to doubt the love of the Father has never really left us. So, to show us the depths of His love by reconciling us to Himself, God sent forth His Son. By His Incarnation, the eternal Son of the Father took on our flesh, born of the Virgin Mary. She, who is unclouded by sin—the Immaculate Conception, listened to the Father and responded in love. By the overshadowing of the Holy Spirit, she conceived in her womb and "the Word became flesh" (John 1:14). Love came down. This is the fulfillment of the promise God first made in the Garden (Genesis 3:15) and the moment that all things begin and are restored in Christ.

Throughout His life, Christ's eyes are always on the Father; His ears are always open to His Word. He models for us what it means to hear and obey the voice of the Father. He invites us to share in His communion with the Father. Made like us in all things but sin, He takes upon Himself the full weight of our sin and nails it to the Cross. As all the ugliness of rejection is hurled at Him on Calvary, His love transforms it into an acceptance of the Father's love. From our posture of rupture, He chooses love. Always obedient, "even unto death" (Philippians 2:8), Jesus Christ conquers death forever by willingly accepting it; turning a tree of death into the tree of life. From His pierced side, blood and water flowed out, His very life given to us through the sacraments. On the third day, Christ rose victorious, conquering sin and death, opening to all who would listen and obey Him the way to eternal life.

Saying "Yes" — Responding in Love

Eternal life is now offered to us, just as it was offered to Adam and Eve in the Garden. Like them, we are endowed with the freedom to listen and accept this gift or reject it. By Baptism, we are immersed into Christ's death and resurrection, "so that as Christ was raised from the dead by the glory of the Father, we too might walk in newness of life" (*CCC*, 654). The restoration established by Christ is shared with us as we are made sons and daughters of God. The theological virtues—faith, hope, and charity—are given to us to reorient us to the Father, equipping us to be in relationship with Him. They empower us to believe Him, to trust Him, and to share in His own divine love. The gifts make us docile and open to the promptings of the Holy Spirit. The sacraments of the Church allow us constant access to Christ so that He remains with us.

> The life of virtue is the life of a disciple of Christ.

The life of virtue, then, is the life of a disciple of Christ who allows Him to bring order and balance back into our lives. Christ won the victory over sin upon the cross. A disciple allows the radiance of that victory to shine on every aspect of his or her life. By God's grace, prudence gives light to our minds, restoring right reason in action. Fortitude and temperance calm the chaos and frustration of our emotions and desires. Justice restores the order of our relationships, rooted in the knowledge that each one of us is known and loved by God.

By responding in love to His grace and striving to live a virtuous life, we are able to heal the interior brokenness caused by sin. The virtues establish within us a firm disposition to pursue goodness and therefore restores inner harmony and freedom. We experience the wholeness each one of us longs for. Our lives have meaning and purpose.

When we have heard Christ, seen Him, touched Him, and experienced the effects of His victory in our lives, not only are we disciples, but we become credible witnesses to Him. We proclaim the Good News by our very lives. We are called to give testimony to the power of God that restores all things in Christ. Give Him access to your heart, hear His call, and experience the happiness of the virtuous life.

Living as a Disciple of Christ

"I came so that they might have life and have it more abundantly."—John 10:10

Beginning at Baptism

The life of a disciple of Christ begins at Baptism, when the new Christian is plunged into the Paschal Mystery: His passion, death, resurrection, and ascension. It is a journey, a pilgrimage to our heavenly homeland. The pattern of dying and rising in Christ marks the life of those seeking to follow in the footsteps of Christ. As we die to sin, not just on the day of our Baptism but every day, Christ raises us to the new life of His grace at work in our lives. Baptism plants the seed of eternal life. Every gift, every grace, every blessing is given to us the moment our souls are freed from original and personal sin and we are reborn as sons and daughters of God.

God, in calling us to communion with Himself as sons and daughters, calls us to a destiny far beyond our natural capacities. "The glory of God is the human being fully alive; the life of man consists in beholding God" (St Irenaeus; *Against Heresies* IV, 20, 7). To enable us to behold Him, He gives us the theological virtues of faith, hope, and charity. These virtues adapt our finite human faculties for participation in the divine life, to be in relationship with God. They infuse and give life to every virtuous action, even the most mundane, allowing human beings to fulfill their mission in the world: to be a sort of "spiritual monstrance of God, wherein the glory of God would break out into the whole creation, shining

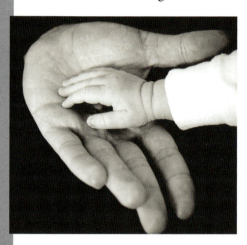

| FAITH | HOPE | LOVE (CHARITY) |

like a radiant spiritual light in the midst of the physical world" (Thomas Joseph White, OP, *Light of Christ*, p. 112).

Restored and Elevated

God's gifts at Baptism are not just for our supernatural life. Christ restores all things, including our humanity because "the glory of God is the human being fully alive." Socrates, Plato, and Aristotle saw in virtue the perfection of human life. Virtue is a habit of doing good, making it easy, delightful. The virtuous human being is free—free to be excellent—not overpowered in any aspect of his life. Each one of us was born with the capacity for virtue, but we need education and practice to attain the freedom, harmony, and balance of the virtuous, excellent human being. That is a daunting task if it centers on our own meager efforts. An aspect of the good news of Christianity is that excellence is not limited to human efforts. In His goodness, God gave us these virtues at Baptism. They are called "cardinal" (from the Latin *cardo*, "hinge") because all the remaining human virtues hinge on these four: prudence, justice, fortitude, and temperance.

> Christ "restores all things," including our humanity.

| PRUDENCE | JUSTICE | FORTITUDE | TEMPERANCE |

Prudence orders our mind and intellect so that we can make right decisions. Justice perfects our will and relationships, ordering them under the rubric of charity. Fortitude and temperance perfect our emotions, either strengthening them in the face of difficulties or moderating them in the pursuit of pleasure. At our Baptism these virtues were given to us as free gifts. When animated by charity and under the prompting of the Holy Spirit, the Christian is empowered to live the natural virtues

Living as a Disciple of Christ

at a higher supernatural pitch. "The goal of the virtuous life is to become like God" (St. Gregory of Nyssa, *CCC*, 1803). Virtue is not just about human flourishing on earth; it is also about living in bliss forever.

God at Work in Us

At our Baptism, the seven gifts of the Holy Spirit were also given to us. They sharpen our faculties, making us receptive to His promptings so He can aid us on our journey to heaven. The seven gifts are seven "ways" the Spirit desires to operate in our lives. Each gift corresponds to a virtue, either flowing from the theological virtues or perfecting the cardinal virtues. John of St. Thomas used the analogy that you can think of our journey to heaven like a man rowing across a lake. Each virtuous action is similar to each pull on the oars. If he has practiced and is an excellent rower, he enjoys his time on the lake and moves steadily. But if the rowboat also has a sail, and the wind is blowing with the rower, he now races along the water. That would be similar to the gifts operating in our lives. Like a properly fitted sail, the gifts make us attuned to the wind of the Holy Spirit. There is an ease and efficacy to the gifts that can only come from the Holy Spirit.

Strengthened, Healed, and Nourished

As the disciple of Christ moves through life, each action is a step, a choice either toward God or away from God. The seed of "newness of life," planted at Baptism, is either allowed to grow and flourish or lie dormant. The Father constantly reaches out to us as He pours upon us the dew of His grace to awaken and sustain this seed.

The new life of Baptism does not abolish the weakness left by original sin. We are left with an inclination toward sin. Living the new life of the baptized is a struggle because the Christian is called to conversion, called to take up his cross daily and follow the crucified Savior (cf. Luke 9:23). There are times when the disciple of Christ turns away from Him, allowing other things to take His place in his or her life. Sin ensnares us, entraps us in its vicious cycle, making it difficult to hear the voice of our Father. Mortal sin cuts us off completely from the life of God and throws us back into the realm of sin and darkness. It is as if a branch cuts itself off the tree, and then withers and dies. "Without me, you can do nothing" (John 15:5). This is no hyperbole, for our God is the source of all life, all grace, all love. Christ, in His great love for us, freely undertook the burden of the cross to free us from the burden of sin. Revelation, particularly the revelation of God's love shown to us on the cross, reveals the seriousness of sin. In the sacrament of Reconciliation, our ruptured relationship with God is restored by Christ. The branch is regrafted onto the tree, so that, once again, the grace of God may be at work in us.

Holy Communion is our "daily bread," effecting an intimate union with Jesus Christ. This daily encounter with Christ preserves, increases, and renews the new life of grace received at Baptism.

The sacrament of Confirmation perfects and strengthens this life of Christ in us, and with this new strength the disciple has an even greater obligation to give witness to Christ and participate

Living as a Disciple of Christ

in His mission. The sacrament of the Eucharist "is a precious nourishment" for this new life, as it is "an encounter with Christ truly present in the supreme act of His love, the life-giving gift of Himself" (*Lumen Fidei*, 44). Holy Communion is our "daily bread," effecting an intimate union with Jesus Christ. This daily encounter with Christ preserves, increases, and renews the new life of grace received at Baptism. When the life of discipleship becomes difficult, turn to Christ in the Eucharist.

Fully Alive

What does it mean to be a disciple of Christ? We have only to look to the "great cloud of witnesses" to see (Hebrews 12:1). The saints are varied and unique, yet all are one in their wholehearted love of Christ and openness to the transformative power of His grace. In them the full riches of the redeeming grace of Christ is on display. They show us how to be Christians, how to live life "fully alive" as God intended. They did not selfishly pursue their own desires; rather they "simply wanted to give themselves, because the light of Christ had shone upon them" (Pope Benedict XVI, 20 August 2005). This is the secret to joy. Made in the image of God—God who is an eternal exchange of self-giving love—the human person will find happiness in the measure that he or she gives himself or herself away (*Gaudium et Spes*, 22). All of us who are baptized belong to this great cloud of witnesses, called to experience the joy of the risen Lord.

The disciple of Christ is rooted in the reality of divine love, knowing that his existence is good and meaningful because he is personally loved, willed, and sustained by God. The disciple knows in the core of her being this truth: "You are a thought of God, you are a heartbeat of God. To say this is like saying that you have a value which in a sense is infinite, that you matter to God in your completely unique individuality" (St. Pope John Paul II, 23 Sept 2001). Turning frequently to Christ in the sacraments, the disciple can intuit that the intimacy of the Garden is not just restored but heightened in these encounters. Adam and Eve may have known the sound of the God's footstep, but they did not rest upon the Lord's heart the way John did at the Last Supper. Adam and Eve spoke with God, but they never received the Lord's Body into their own the way we can each day at Mass. When God promised salvation amidst that initial pain of sin, no one could have imagined that the salvation would not just equal but far exceed anything Adam and Eve ever experienced. How can the disciple of Christ respond with anything less than his whole being, his whole life? Christ came so that we may have abundant life (cf. John 10:10). Say "yes" to His gift!

This is the secret to joy. Made in the image of God—God who is an eternal exchange of self-giving love—the human person will find happiness in the measure that he or she gives himself or herself away (Gaudium et Spes, 22)

Section 2 | What Are the Virtues?

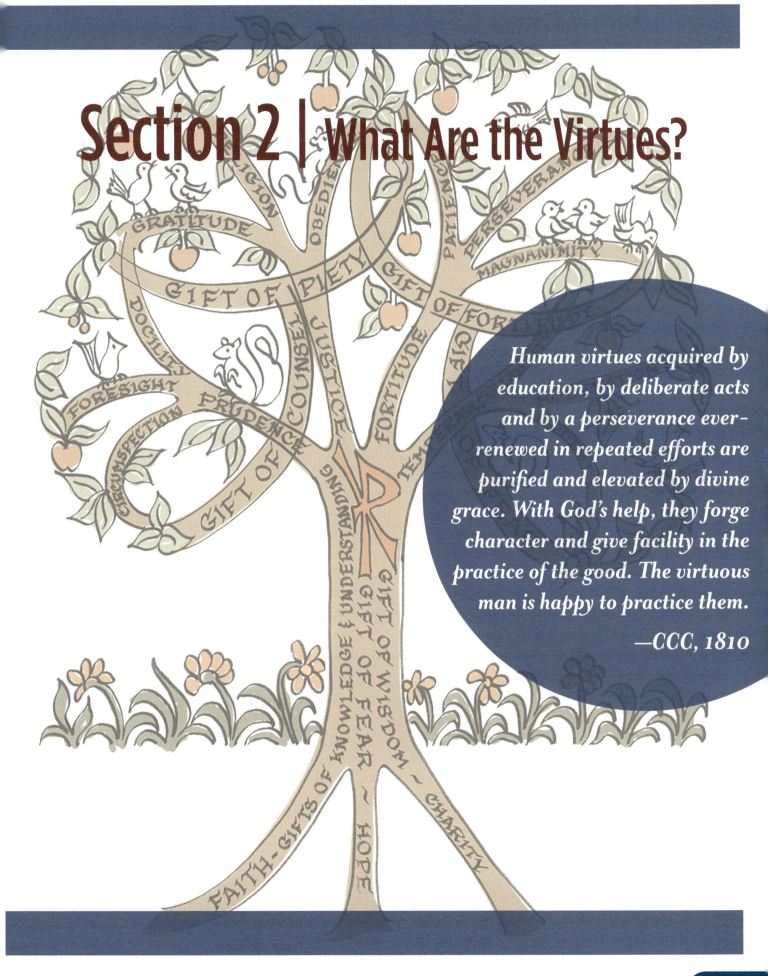

> *Human virtues acquired by education, by deliberate acts and by a perseverance ever-renewed in repeated efforts are purified and elevated by divine grace. With God's help, they forge character and give facility in the practice of the good. The virtuous man is happy to practice them.*
>
> —CCC, 1810

The Road Map...

VIRTUE PAGES

Each virtue page explains the Theological (Faith, Hope, and Charity) and Cardinal (Prudence, Justice, Fortitude, and Temperance) virtues by breaking the virtue down into the following sections:

KNOW IT

In order to live as a disciple of Christ, one must first learn the meaning of the virtues and gifts of the Holy Spirit. The "Know It" section provides the definitions of the virtue and key points about how to cultivate them in one's life.

PRAY IT

Prayer is simply a conversation with God. Prayerfully reading Scripture *(lectio divina)* enables us to know Him and intensifies our desire to live in friendship with Him.

GUARD IT

The virtues and the gifts are infused by God, but we must guard these gifts given to us. Self-knowledge is essential to living a virtuous life. An honest examination of conscience is the surest means of guarding one's relationship with God. Seeking forgiveness enables Him to restore the beauty of His image and likeness in us.

LIVE IT

Disciples of Christ live differently. His grace in us enables us to trust God for our salvation, confidently anchoring us in God. This truth gives us a firm purpose in life and empowers us to live freely as His disciples. Our world view is different because we have seen Him, touched Him, and heard Him (cf. 1 John 1:1–14). This experience impels us to be credible witnesses, joyfully proclaiming by our lives the One whom we love.

GO DEEPER

At the end of each section on the theological and cardinal virtues, there is the "Going Deeper" section. This section has additional information on the virtue, such as related topics, opposing vices, or references from the *Catechism of the Catholic Church* or Church documents.

RELATED VIRTUES PAGES

Following each cardinal virtue (Prudence, Justice, Fortitude, and Temperance), there is a section on the virtues "related" to that cardinal virtue (*for the listing of related virtues, see page 19*). Related virtue pages are broken down as follows:

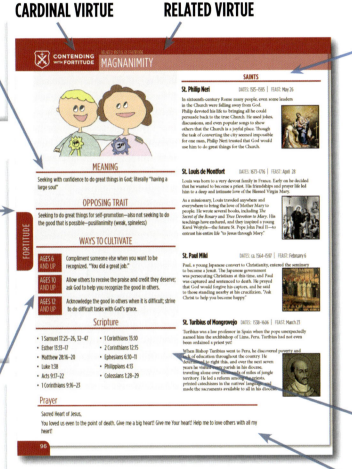

VIRTUE MEANING provides a simple definition of the virtue.

OPPOSING TRAIT gives examples of the opposite vice. If people find themselves acting this way, they know what virtue to practice to overcome that fault.

WAYS TO CULTIVATE offers age level suggestions and practical ways to cultivate growth in virtue. These suggestions are rooted in ways to dispose oneself to God's grace while developing good habits.

SAINTS are our models and intercessors in the Christian life. They were canonized because of their heroic practice of virtue. They are our older brothers and sisters in the family of God and are ever ready to support us in our pursuit of virtue. These short vignettes of the saints are meant to illustrate each virtue and to inspire us to practice it in our lives.

SCRIPTURE passages about the virtue are listed.

PRAYER: "God gives the growth" (1 Corinthians 3:7), so any authentic growth in virtue is dependent on His grace. This short prayer gives words to the aspirations of one who is trying to growth in this virtue.

17

The Virtues and Gifts

THEOLOGICAL VIRTUES

Supernatural gifts infused by God at Baptism which directly relate to Him and dispose one to live in relationship with the Father, the Son, and the Holy Spirit

 Faith enables one to know God and all that He has revealed

 Hope enables one to desire God above all things and to trust Him for our salvation

 Charity enables one to love God above all and to love our neighbor as ourselves

GIFTS OF THE HOLY SPIRIT

Infused by God at Baptism, the gifts, in conjunction with the virtues, make one receptive to the inspirations of the Holy Spirit (see Isaiah 11:1–2)

WISDOM

- The gift of Wisdom moves one to order one's life according to God's will.
- *Perfects the theological virtue of Charity*

COUNSEL

- The gift of Counsel enables one to respond fully to the direction and guidance from the Lord.
- *Perfects the cardinal virtue of Prudence*

FORTITUDE

- The gift of Fortitude moves one to endure difficulties for the sake of eternal life with God.
- *Perfects the cardinal virtue of Fortitude*

PIETY

- The gift of Piety inclines one as a child of God to have devotion and honor to God as Father.
- *Perfects the cardinal virtue of Justice*

UNDERSTANDING

- The gift of Understanding enables one to see more deeply into the mysteries of the faith and to judge with certainty all created things.
- *Perfects the theological virtue of Faith*

KNOWLEDGE

- The Gift of Knowledge guides one in knowing what to believe and how to share it with others.
- *Perfects the theological virtue of Faith*

FEAR OF THE LORD

- The gift of Fear of the Lord brings forth the fear of offending God by sin.
- *Perfects the theological virtue of Hope and the cardinal virtue of Temperance*

 The practice of all of the virtues is animated and inspired by charity, which "Binds everything together in perfect harmony." —Colossians 3:14, CCC, 1827

Fruits of the Spirit

Charity	Generosity
Joy	Gentleness
Peace	Faithfulness
Patience	Modesty
Kindness	Self-Control
Goodness	Chastity

GOD GIVES THE GROWTH—1 Corinthians 3:7

CARDINAL VIRTUES
Pivotal habits of right thinking, ordering of the passions, and moral conduct which aim to perfect human living

(Sound Judgment)

Prudence enables one to reason and to act rightly in any given situation—"right reason in action."

(Fairness)

Justice enables one to give to each, beginning with God, what is due him.

(Courage)

Fortitude enables one to endure difficulties and pain for the sake of what is good.

(Self-Control)

Temperance enables one to be moderate in the pleasure and use of created goods.

—RELATED VIRTUES—

Circumspection	Affability	Obedience	Industriousness	Honesty
Docility	Courtesy	Patriotism	Magnanimity	Humility
Foresight	Generosity	Prayerfulness	Magnificence	Meekness
	Gratitude	Respect	Patience	Moderation
	Kindness	Sincerity	Perseverance	Modesty
	Loyalty	Trustworthiness		Orderliness
				Self-Control

The goal of a virtuous life is to become like God

—St. Gregory of Nyssa

—By God's grace, prudence gives light to our minds, restoring right reason in action. Fortitude and temperance calm the chaos and frustration of our emotions and desires. Justice restores the order of our relationships, rooted in the knowledge that each one of us is known and loved by God.—

—VIRTUES, GIFTS, BEATITUDES—

VIRTUES	GIFTS	BEATITUDES
FAITH	Understanding & Knowledge	Pure of Heart, those who weep
HOPE	Fear of the Lord	Poor in Spirit
CHARITY	Wisdom	Peacemakers
PRUDENCE	Counsel	The Merciful
JUSTICE	Piety	The Meek
FORTITUDE	Fortitude	Hunger and thirst for justice
TEMPERANCE	Fear of the Lord	Poor in spirit

19

The Virtue Tree Diagram

THE GOAL OF A VIRTUOUS LIFE IS TO BECOME LIKE GOD. — ST. GREGORY OF NYSSA

The Virtue Tree

This virtue tree is a fitting metaphor for the life of virtue. Just as the roots of a tree hold it in place, so do the theological virtues root us in God. "Charity is like the sap that nourishes the trunk and rises into the branches, the network of virtues, to produce the delicious fruit of good works. It is through this new love revealed and shared in Christ that the Holy Spirit works in us" (Servais Pinkaers, OP, *Morality: The Catholic View*, St. Augustine's Press, 2003, 87). The four main trunks of the tree represent the cardinal virtues upon which all good habits hinge. When we are open to the grace of God at work in us through the gifts and virtues, we are able to flourish. A thriving tree soon becomes a home to birds and small animals. The person fully alive in Christ is able to welcome others, sharing with them the riches he or she has received.

SEEING WITH FAITH

FAITH

Faith, usually represented by an eye, is the theological virtue by which one is able to "see" God in the spiritual sense. This virtue gives the conviction that all God has revealed through Sacred Scripture and Tradition is true.

If we look with the eyes of faith, things look different than they do in the natural realm. For example, if we see a child who is sick, we might only notice the suffering and be very sad. But with the eyes of faith, we see in the sick child an image of the suffering Christ.

"Faith is the realization of what is hoped for and evidence of things not seen."

—*Hebrews 11:1*

FAITH

KNOW IT

Theological Virtue of Faith

CCC, 1814–1816

CCC, 2656

Faith

CCC, 142–175

Transmission of Divine Revelation

CCC, 74–95

Sins Opposed to Faith

CCC, 2087–2089

Summa Theologiae

II–II.Q47, St. Thomas Aquinas

Echoing the Mystery

10–Faith

FAITH enables one to know God and all that He has revealed.

Faith is a theological virtue, a supernatural gift of God infused at Baptism. It a free gift of the Holy Spirit that moves the heart and opens the eyes of the mind to God, enabling us to say "I believe." It is an assent first to God Himself, to all that He has revealed and that the Church proposes for our belief. This assent is certain, complete, and confident, firmly rooted in knowledge of the Father's love. By faith, we freely commit our entire self to God (*Dei Verbum*, 5), beginning a path upon which we seek to know and do the Father's will.

God, in His goodness, created us for a supernatural end—to be happy with Him forever. **Divine Revelation** is God's communication of Himself, His love, and His plan for our salvation. He speaks to us, guides us, sharing with us "the deepest truth about God and the salvation of man" shining out for our sake in Christ (*Dei Verbum*, 2). All that He has revealed has been entrusted to the Church. This deposit of faith is known to us by **Scripture, Tradition,** and guarded by the **Magisterium**.

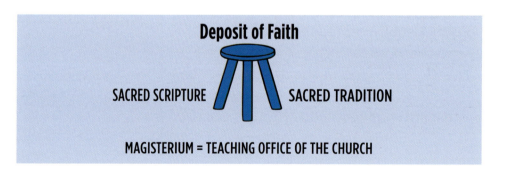

Key Points

- Faith is a supernatural gift of God infused at Baptism.
- It enables one to believe in God.
- It enables one to believe all that God has said and revealed to us in Divine Revelation.

24

GUARD IT

FAITH

The theological virtue of Faith enables one to know God and all He has revealed. It sanctifies human intelligence and enables one to be united to God. In order to guard our faith, one must actively strive to nourish it. This is done by observing the first commandment of God's law of love: "To love the Lord our God with all our heart, and with all our soul, and with all our mind." It is also nourished by the following:

Prayer enables us to guard our heart by living in communion with God.

Reception of the Sacraments, especially the Eucharist and Reconciliation, nourishes our soul with His life and grace.

Study of the truth contained in the Deposit of Faith.

Ways to sin against Faith include the following:

Voluntary	The deliberate refusal to believe what God has revealed either directly (divine revelation) or through the Church (*CCC*, 2087–2089)
Incredulity	Willfully neglecting the truths of the Faith
Heresy	The denial of some aspect of the Faith
Apostasy	Complete abandonment of the Christian Faith
Schism	Refusal to submit to the Pope or to be visibly united to the Catholic Church

> *Faith tells us that God has given His Son for our sakes and gives us the victorious certainty that it is really true: God is love!*
> —Pope Benedict XVI

> *Faith…is assenting to a doctrine as true, which we do not see, which we cannot prove, because God says it is true, who cannot lie.*
> —John Henry Cardinal Newman

> Jesus said to them in reply, "Have faith in God."
> —Mark 11:22

> For I am not ashamed of the gospel. It is the power of God for the salvation of everyone who believes: for Jew first, and then Greek.
>
> For in it is revealed the righteousness of God from faith to faith; as it is written, "The one who is righteous by faith will live."
> —Romans 1:16–17

FAITH

KNOW IT

RELATED BEATITUDE

The Gift of Understanding

"Blessed are the pure of heart, for they shall see God." —Matthew 5:8

The pure of heart are singularly given over to God and as a result, they are promised the joy of seeing God. Understanding helps man to see more clearly the truths related to God.

Summa Theologiae

II–II.Q8, St. Thomas Aquinas

The Gift of Knowledge

"Blessed are those who mourn, for they shall be comforted." —Matthew 5:4

The chief sense of mourning is the sorrow that comes from sin. One of the greatest sources of knowledge for man is the knowledge one gains from making mistakes and repenting of them.

Summa Theologiae

II–II.Q9–16, St. Thomas Aquinas

UNDERSTANDING enables one to see more deeply into the mysteries of the faith and to judge with certainty all created things.

By the theological virtue of Faith, we are given the grace to believe the mysteries of the Faith. The **Gift of Understanding** helps us penetrate the mysteries, lifting the veil of obscurity even here on earth. This understanding is not so much the fruit of study, but of love, a sort of connaturality with God's understanding. The gift of understanding allows the Christian to grasp first principles, the organic unity of all truths, so he or she is able to act in a way that is marked by integrity and consistency.

KNOWLEDGE guides one in knowing what to believe and how to share it with others.

The theological virtue of faith gives us the grace to know God, to believe Him and to believe all that He has revealed. The **Gift of Knowledge** is rooted in faith, and from this firm foundation, gives the disciple the ability to look at the world and see all of creation as God's handiwork. It opens our eyes to see the Creator manifested in His creation. Under the influence of the Holy Spirit, the disciple is able to judge rightly created things in relation to his or her supernatural destiny.

Effects of the Gift of the Holy Spirit

Gift of Understanding

- Gives one deeper insight into the meaning of Scripture, the truths of the Faith, moral teachings
- Imparts a sense of confidence and certainty in belief
- Grasps the reality of heaven, our beatific communion with God
- Reveals how the truths of Faith serve as standards for human actions

Gift of Knowledge

- Discerns the relation of created things to one's heavenly goal
- Sees God's divine attributes reflected in created realities
- Knows what to believe and how to share it with others
- Gives certitude in matters of the practice of the Faith
- Instills confidence in the pursuit of truth, both the truths of faith and of science

GUARD IT

FAITH

The theological virtue of Faith and the Gifts of Understanding and Knowledge are gifts given us at Baptism. Like any gift, they must be guarded. It is important to know about potential sins or vices which weaken or diminish the ability to live in the Spirit. The sins opposed to the Gifts of Knowledge and Understanding are rooted in the capital sins of lust and gluttony.

There are two capital sins that impede the Gifts of Understanding and Knowledge:

- **Lust:** The pleasures of the senses, particularly sexuality, are powerful, and when overindulged have the ability to cloud or even blind our minds to the truths of faith. Lust can cause a **blindness of the mind,** preventing one from thinking clearly, and causing one to lose the taste for spiritual goods. The faculties of the soul become inverted, with the emotions leading the will and clouding the mind.

  Living a life of purity is a remedy to blindness of mind. Those who are "pure in heart" can "see God" because they manifest an integrated life in three ways:

  1) Life of charity
  2) Life of chastity
  3) Life committed to the truth

- **Gluttony:** The pleasures of food and drink have a dulling effect when overindulged. Someone's mind is "sharp" when it can quickly pierce to reality. Understanding sharpens one's mind to pierce to the essence of truth. Gluttony is an undue attachment to the pleasures of food and drink. Therefore, it weakens one's understanding of spiritual things and causes a **dullness of sense**, particularly one's spiritual senses. Gluttony, according to St. Thomas, is not just overeating. It can manifest itself in five ways: too soon, too expensively, too much, too eagerly, too fastidiously.

> *Lust is the isolation of sex from true love. There is no passion that more quickly produces slavery than lust—as there is none whose perversions more quickly destroy the power of the intellect and the will.*
> —Venerable Fulton Sheen, Lift Up Your Heart, A Guide to Spiritual Peace

> *When men begin to forget their souls, they begin to take great care of their bodies. There are more athletic clubs in the modern world than there are spiritual retreat houses; and who shall count the millions spent in beauty shops to glorify faces that will one day be the prey of worms?*
> —Venerable Fulton Sheen, Victory Over Vice

> *For the LORD gives wisdom, from his mouth come knowledge and understanding.*
> —Proverbs 2:6

FAITH

PRAY IT *LECTIO DIVINA*

Matthew 20:29–34

As they left Jericho, a great crowd followed him. Two blind men were sitting by the roadside, and when they heard that Jesus was passing by, they cried out, "[Lord,] Son of David, have pity on us!" The crowd warned them to be silent, but they called out all the more, "Lord, Son of David, have pity on us!" Jesus stopped and called them and said, "What do you want me to do for you?" They answered him, "Lord, let our eyes be opened." Moved with pity, Jesus touched their eyes. Immediately they received their sight, and followed him.

1. God's Word strikes the heart. What word or phrase touched your heart?
2. The two blind men were unable to physically see Jesus. How did they know He was passing by?
3. Describe the actions of the two blind men.
4. How did Jesus respond when He noticed the blind men?
5. Ask this question in prayer: "Jesus, Son of David, the blind men first saw You with the eyes of faith. How can I be a better witness to the faith when people try to silence me?" Write down what He says to you.

PRAY IT

Pray an Act of Faith

O My God,

I firmly believe that You are one God in three divine Persons, Father, Son, and Holy Spirit. I believe that Your divine Son became man and died for our sins, and that He will come to judge the living and the dead. I believe these and all the truths which the holy Catholic Church teaches, because in revealing them You can neither deceive nor be deceived.

FAITH

LIVE IT — LOOKING TO THE SAINTS

VEN. FULTON SHEEN

Peter John Sheen was born on an Illinois farm in 1895. He was called "Fulton," his mother's maiden name. When he was young, the family moved to Peoria. There, he graduated with honors from high school at Spalding Institute. He was ordained a priest in 1919.

> **Seeing with Faith**
>
> He had the ability to make the deep truths of the Faith clear and understandable.

It was obvious to Father Sheen's bishop that this young priest was very intelligent. He also had a lively faith. He began everyday with a holy hour before the Blessed Sacrament and was already showing signs of the passion for evangelization that would mark his later life. The bishop sent him to the Catholic University of America (CUA) in Washington, D.C. But his professors recommended him to study in Europe. The following year he went to the Catholic University of Louvain in Belgium and then after that to the Angelicum in Rome. He came back to the States and began teaching at Catholic University of America.

Over the next twenty three years, Father Sheen taught philosophy and theology at CUA. His lectures became very popular with students and visitors alike. He worked hard on his presentations, often spending hours working on them. His oratory skills were extraordinary, making people feel like he was speaking directly to them. He had the ability to make the deep truths of the Faith clear and understandable.

Throughout his life, Sheen was an ardent evangelist. He began broadcasting on the radio in 1926. In 1930 he became a weekly speaking on The Catholic Hour radio program. Over the next 20 years, he spoke on a range of topics: from the Real Presence of the Eucharist, to devotion to Our Lady, to moral theology and the practical decisions of daily life. His lively faith opened him up to the Spirit's gifts of knowledge and understanding, allowing him to reach all types of people. In 1940 he participated in the first televised broadcast of a religious service. By this point, he had achieved incredible fame as an orator, speaker, author, and Catholic evangelist.

In 1950 he left CUA because he was appointed the director of the Society for the Propagation of the Faith. Soon, two things happened. Sheen was consecrated a bishop and he began his television series Life is Worth Living. Over the next 16 years, the series would run on DuMont Television Network and then ABC. This series tackled spiritual, philosophical, moral, and religious issues that were relevant to the times. He also addressed current events, particularly Communism, and help people understand them in light of Catholic teaching.

In 1952, Bishop Sheen won the Emmy Award for Most Outstanding Television Personality. It is estimated that up to 10 million viewers watched his show each week.

Archbishop Sheen was a sort of grandfather of the New Evangelization. Long before St. Pope John Paul II called for new methods, new expressions, and new ardor at the service of the Gospel, Fulton Sheen was doing just that. As media developed, he was there, ready to use it to spread the Faith. He was always ready to engage people in a conversation, yet never gave up his convictions and devotion to the truth. His firm faith was a rock upon which and from which he was able to dialogue with the world. He is a model of the New Evangelization and people engage the media and its technology to spread the Good News of Jesus Christ.

FAITH

LIVE IT

FAITH enables one to know God and all that He has revealed.

A Disciple of Christ living the virtue of faith...

- ✓ Regularly receives the sacraments.
- ✓ Reads and meditates on the Word of God.
- ✓ Cultivates friendship with God in prayer.
- ✓ Professes in words and deeds.
- ✓ Seeks to know and understand what God has revealed.
- ✓ Courageously shares the faith with others.
- ✓ Confidently bears witness to Christ in daily life.

The Disciple of Christ...

The disciple of Christ must not only keep the faith and live on it, but also profess it, confidently bear witness to it, and spread it: "All however must be prepared to confess Christ before men and to follow him along the way of the Cross, amidst the persecutions which the Church never lacks." Service of and witness to the faith are necessary for salvation: "So every one who acknowledges me before men, I also will acknowledge before my Father who is in heaven; but whoever denies me before men, I also will deny before my Father who is in heaven." (CCC, 1816)

Going Deeper in Faith

FAITH

FROM THE CATECHISM

Faith is the theological virtue by which we believe in God and believe all that he has said and revealed to us, and that Holy Church proposes for our belief, because he is truth itself. By faith "man freely commits his entire self to God." For this reason the believer seeks to know and do God's will (*CCC*, 1814).

- **Faith and reason are not contradictory.** The God who made us is the same God who speaks to us, who calls us to respond to Him in faith. Faith and reason are two complementary modes of knowing the truths of the faith never contradict the truths of reason.

"Even if faith is superior to reason there can never be a true divergence between faith and reason, since the same God who reveals the mysteries and bestows the gift of faith has also placed in the human spirit the light of reason. God could not deny himself, nor could the truth ever contradict the truth" (*Fides et Ratio*, 53; quoting Vatican II's *Dei Filius*, 4).

"If methodical investigation within every branch of learning is carried out in a genuinely scientific manner and in accord with moral norms, it never truly conflicts with faith, for earthly matters and the concerns of faith derive from the same God. Indeed whoever labors to penetrate the secrets of reality with a humble and steady mind, even though he is unaware of the fact, is nevertheless being led by the hand of God, who holds all things in existence, and gives them their identity" (Vatican II's *Gaudium et Spes*, 36; see also *CCC*, 159).

- **The Obedience of Faith (see *CCC*, 144–149)**

The obedience of faith (cf. Romans 13:26; 1:5; 2 Corinthians 10:5–6) "is to be given to God who reveals, an obedience by which man commits his whole self freely to God, offering the full submission of intellect and will to God who reveals, and freely assenting to the truth revealed by Him" (Vatican II's *Dei Verbum*, 5; see also *CCC*, 143).

Mary, the new Eve, perfectly embodied the obedience of faith. Eve listened to the voice of the serpent, doubted and disobeyed God. Mary heard the voice of God and in faith obeyed Him. We, too, are called to listen in order to know and do God's will.

The Blessed Virgin Mary and the Gifts of the Holy Spirit

"Who Is My Mother?" — The Gift of Understanding

When the crowd tells Jesus that his Mother and brothers are outside waiting to see him, Jesus responds: "Who are my mother and my brothers? Whoever does the will of God is brother and sister and mother to me. My mother and brothers are those who hear the word of God and act upon it" (see also Mark 3:33, 35, Luke 8:21). By his response, the Lord reveals a new understanding to his disciples, an understanding that continues to be given to Christians by the Holy Spirit as his divine Gift.

Understanding implies a certain intimate knowing. To understand or to exercise intelligence is to "read within." God understands that the natural light of our human understanding is of limited power and can go only so far. That is why he graces us with the supernatural light of the Gift of Understanding by which we penetrate to the supernatural happiness and communion with God for which we were made.

By his answer, Jesus enlightens the crowd of their need to reach beyond their own preset notions, conceptions, and prejudices to certain deeper truths that only the Holy Spirit can reveal. If we do so in love, then the Spirit's Gift of Understanding gives us a certain excellence of knowledge that inwardly penetrates to the very things of God. At the same time, the Spirit transforms the way we regard and assess ourselves. The divine Gift of Understanding illumines us to see how Christ reveals us to ourselves. We could not even understand ourselves correctly without the grace of his Understanding.

The special value of the Gift of Understanding lies in the way it considers eternal and necessary truths as reliable rules for human conduct. The Gift of Understanding leads us to perform divinely directed human actions. That is why the true "mother" of God is one who devotedly does God's will (cf. Matthew 12:50, Mark 3:35). In such a one, understanding and action form an organic, integral, life-giving whole. And as we do God's will, the Holy Spirit enables us to see beyond the immediate implications of our actions and to apprehend the truth about our final end with God. Therefore, the purpose of the Gift of Understanding is to give us a sureness of faith regarding our identity before God and the way that we belong to him.

The Gift of Understanding works in concert with the Beatitude of purity of heart (cf. Matthew 5:8). For we cannot worthily receive the truth about God—or the truth about ourselves as brothers, sisters, and mother of Jesus—unless we are spiritually "clean." Such cleanness is the result of the Gift of Understanding.

The Lord's response to the crowd is in no way a slight or insult to the Blessed Mother. For Mary is one who ardently wants us to share in the intimate understanding of the Holy Spirit. She deliberately comes to the crowd—and she comes into our life—so that as we are prompted to remind Jesus of Mary's presence, the Lord in turn will be moved to bless us with that divine understanding by which we share in the blessedness of his Mother, the first to hear the Word of God who is Jesus and to act upon it.

"The Blessed Virgin Mary And The Gifts Of The Holy Spirit," pg. 31. Cameron, Peter John O.P. *The Gifts of the Holy Spirit*. Veritas Series. Connecticut: Knights of Columbus, 2002.

The Blessed Virgin Mary and the Gifts of the Holy Spirit

The Presentation in the Temple and the Gift of Knowledge

Joseph and Mary present the infant Jesus in the temple so as to fulfill the law of Moses by offering sacrifice "in accord with the dictate of the law of the Lord" (Luke 2:23). They manifest in their offering the Spirit's Gift of Knowledge. For the Gift of Knowledge enables us to know what we ought to believe and do regarding God by giving us discernment about what belongs to the matter of faith. The Gift of Knowledge provides sure and correct judgment about the things of faith. And so, in obedience of faith, Mary and Joseph present Jesus to God in the temple.

There they encounter the "pious and just" man Simeon (Luke 2:25). The Holy Spirit has graced him with a very special knowledge: "that he would not experience death until he had seen the Anointed of the Lord" (Luke 2:26). But the trouble is this: How would Simeon know the Messiah when he appeared? It is the Spirit's Gift of Knowledge that blesses Simeon with sure and correct judgment about the identity of Jesus as he sees the Lord with Mary and Joseph. The Gift of Knowledge moves Simeon to the conviction that the baby Mary gives him to hold in his arms is the very object of his faith. Mary gives us Jesus as well so that we too can hold him close, so that he might renew and revive our flagging faith.

Simeon recognizes God Incarnate in the human flesh of Jesus through the supernatural assistance of the Gift of Knowledge. The impulse of that gift stirs Simeon in turn to express his certitude and conviction: "Now, Master, you have fulfilled your word. For my eyes have witnessed your salvation" (Luke 2:29–30). The Gift of Knowledge gives us a graced way of discerning. It enables us to look upon created things and to assess with certainty, how they bolster our belief and feed our life of faith. Because of the Gift of Knowledge, we regard and esteem the presence and action of God in creation in a new way: with the "revealing light to the Gentiles" (Luke 2:31). This experience also blesses Mary with new knowledge. Simeon assures her: "You yourself shall be pierced with a sword so that the thoughts of many hearts may be laid bare" (Luke 2:35). The Blessed Mother's participation in the redemptive mission of her Son will cause many to empty their lives of old thoughts and ideas so as to make room for the Spirit's Gift of Knowledge, a knowledge of the Truth that transforms us by uniting us to the very mind and heart of God. God gives Mary to us as a Mother with whom we can lay bare our hearts and unburden our souls. As we confide ourselves to Mary's maternal care, she invites us to the Truth that liberates us, that brings full meaning and value to our life, that fills our life with peace. By our union with Mary, the Spouse of the Holy Spirit, the Spirit's Gift of Knowledge comes to fruition within us.

Anna the Prophetess also confirms the sure and correct judgment the gift of knowledge renders regarding the infant Jesus as she talks about the child "to all who looked forward to deliverance" (cf. Luke 2:36–38). We are part of her audience; the Spirit's Gift of Knowledge gives us ears to hear, to listen, to believe, to respond in faith.

We are told that the child Jesus "grew in size and strength, filled with wisdom, and the grace of God was upon him" (Luke 2:40). Through the Gift of Knowledge, we can be certain that we will grow likewise. And the Blessed Mother will remain as instrumental in our own process of growth as she was in the life of her Son, Jesus.

"The Presentation in the Temple and the Gift of Knowledge", pg. 34. Cameron, Peter John O.P. *The Gifts of the Holy Spirit*. Veritas Series. Connecticut: Knights of Columbus, 2002.

ABIDING WITH HOPE

HOPE

Hope can be represented by an anchor because it firmly roots our desires and lives in God. Once a captain navigates his way to his destination, the anchor keeps the ship firmly in the desired place. We are captains of our own lives. Whatever storms we may have to endure on our way to our final destination in heaven, hope will anchor us strongly inside the Church with Christ.

"This we have as an anchor of the soul, sure and firm, which reaches into the interior behind the veil, where Jesus has entered on our behalf as forerunner, becoming high priest forever according to the order of Melchizedek."

—Hebrews 6:19-20

HOPE

KNOW IT

HOPE enables one to desire God above all things and to trust Him for personal salvation.

Hope is a theological virtue, a supernatural gift from God infused at Baptism. Hope is rooted in the fact that our Creator loved us into being, continually sustains us by His love, and accomplished our salvation by the death and resurrection of Jesus. In the face of this divine love, hope gives confidence, freedom, joy, and assurance to the Christian. "I belong to Christ, I am not alone." By hope we desire heaven, placing trust in Jesus Christ and not in our own strength. This virtue responds to the deepest aspirations of the human heart, assuring us that Jesus is the "answer to the question posed by every human life" (St. Pope John Paul II, October 8, 1995).

This virtue keeps us oriented toward our final destiny, eternal life with the Trinity. It is the virtue of the pilgrim who lives in joyful expectation of eternal beatitude. This virtue inspires us to direct our actions toward God above all else. In this way it preserves us from selfishness, keeps us from discouragement, and sustains us through trials. Hope is "the distinguishing mark of Christians;" they know "their lives will not end in emptiness"; they have a future in God (cf. *Spe Salvi*, 2).

The virtues related to hope are **magnanimity** and **humility**. The magnanimous person seeks to do great things for God. When coupled with the virtue of humility, the disciple recognizes that all good things come from God. The humble and magnanimous person is free to see and rejoice in the gifts of others.

Theological Virtue of Hope
CCC, 1817–1821

CCC, 1843

Heaven
CCC, 1023–1029

Sins Against Hope
CCC, 2090–2092

CCC, 2733

Summa Theologiae
II–II.Q17–18, 20–22 St. Thomas Aquinas

Echoing the Mystery
39–Hope

Key Points

- Hope is a supernatural gift of God infused at Baptism
- Hope anchors the soul in God and enables one to keep their eyes fixed on heaven
- Hope frees us from discouragement, selfishness, and gives a youthful freedom and joy

GUARD IT

HOPE

The theological virtue of hope anchors us in God. Hope is the virtue of a beloved child who confidentially trusts in His love. It also gives us a filial trust in our heavenly Father. In order to guard hope, we must strengthen our resolve to trust in God's loving mercy.

Prayer, **reception of the sacraments**, and the practice of the **presence of God** are some ways to nourish hope. We must also guard it by honestly recognizing sins which directly diminish or weaken hope. The two primary sins against hope are presumption and despair.

- **Presumption:** Taking advantage of God's goodness

There are two kinds of presumption. In the first, a person presumes on his own capacities. He believes owns works can merit salvation, that he does not need God's help.

In the ancient world, Pelagius popularized this idea, teaching that we could live a good life without grace. In the second, a person presumes upon God's goodness and mercy. He believes that God's love is so great, that he does not need to according to any moral norms to be prepared for heaven.

PRESUMPTION	
Presuming on one's capacities for salvation	Presuming on God's mercy for salvation
This person does not see the need for God's grace to get to heaven. To justify his autonomous behavior, he might say something like, "I am a good person; of course I'm going to go to heaven."	This person thinks that everyone will go to heaven because a good God would not send anyone to hell. They fail to make the connection between the choices we make in this life and our final choice to either accept or reject God.
(See the parable of the Pharisee in Luke 18:9–14)	*(See the parable of the wedding feast in Matthew 22:1–14)*

- **Despair:** Giving up on God's goodness

By the sin of despair, a person gives up on the possibility of salvation. He believes his sin is too grievous to merit God's forgiveness, or that it is impossible to overcome his sins even with God's aid. It is not just an overwhelming emotion; it is a conscious decision, engaging both the intellect and the will, that salvation is in some way, impossible.

DESPAIR	
God will not provide what is necessary for salvation.	God will not forgive the sins I have committed.
Contrast Judas and Peter's reactions to their sins of betrayal. *(See Matthew 26:69–79 [Peter] and Matthew 27:3–11 [Judas])*	

> *The saints were able to make the great journey of human existence in the way that Christ had done before them, because they were brimming with great hope.*
> —Pope Benedict XVI, Spe Salvi, 39

> *Heaven is a city on a hill, Hence, we cannot coast into it; we have to climb it. Those who are too lazy to mount can miss its capture as well as the evil who refuse to see it. Let no one think he can be totally indifferent to God in this life and suddenly develop a capacity for Him at the moment of death.*
> —Venerable Fulton Sheen, Victory Over Vice

> *The Christian who despairs about eternal life not only destroys the pilgrim character of his natural existence but also denies the actual "way" to eternal happiness and fulfillment: Christ himself… For the Christian, despair is a decision against Christ. It is a denial of the redemption.*
> —Josef Pieper, Faith Hope Love

> *Rejoice in hope, endure in affliction, persevere in prayer.*
> —Romans 12:12

HOPE

KNOW IT

GIFT OF FEAR OF THE LORD

RELATED BEATITUDE

The Gift of Fear of the Lord

"Blessed are the poor in spirit, for theirs is the kingdom of heaven."
—Matthew 5:3

The Gift of Fear of the Lord enables one to seek God Himself as one's only treasure. By living the beatitude "poor in spirit," one is freed from greed and pride.

Summa Theologiae

II–II.Q19, 22, St. Thomas Aquinas

Fear of the Lord brings forth the fear of offending God by sin.

By the virtue of hope, we are given the grace to trust God for our salvation. Hope is the virtue of the pilgrim, of one on a journey to our heavenly home, to be with our Father who loves us. Sin is turning away, going in the wrong direction, moving away from the Father. The **Gift of Fear of the Lord** gives us a real horror of sin, not because we are afraid of punishment, but because it is a turning away from all that is good. It is "filial," the fear of a child who is confident in the love of his parents. Nurtured by this love, the child develops his talents, does his best to do well, and avoids anything that would offend his parents.

We normally use the word "fear" to describe an emotion. St. Thomas noted that there are **four ways we speak of fear.** The last, filial fear, is the context in which we speak about this gift of the Holy Spirit.

1. **Worldly Fear:** Love of the things of the world and fear of the loss of those goods
2. **Servile Fear:** Fear of the punishment as the principle motive for avoiding sin
3. **Initial Fear:** Moving toward filial fear, while still influenced by a fear of punishment
4. **Filial Fear:** The gift of the Holy Spirit that makes one revere God and avoid sin out of love for Him

Effects of the Gift of the Holy Spirit

- Awakens the horror and sorrow for sin because it is a loss of friendship with God
- Gives firm resolve to do the Father's will
- Instills reverence, awe, humility
- Gives vigilance in avoiding sin and occasions of sin

GUARD IT

HOPE

The theological virtue of hope and the gift of fear of the Lord are given us at Baptism. Like any gift, these must be guarded from sins or vices which may prevent us from desiring God and trusting in Him.

- **Pride:** By hope, we trust in God. By pride, we trust in ourselves, leading us to disregard the commands of God that lead us toward salvation. It is an excessive self-esteem or self-love by which we desire attention, honor, or status beyond what is true. It leads to unnecessary competition internally, with others, and even with God Himself, closing off one's self to God's love and the generosity of His plan for our salvation.

Fear of the Lord aids us in avoiding sin, protecting our relationship with God.

From his earliest years, St. Dominic Savio had a true horror of sin borne of his great love for God. He wrote these resolutions in a prayer book on the occasion of his First Holy Communion at the age of seven.

1. I shall go to confession often, and I shall receive Holy Communion as often as the confessor will permit.
2. I want to keep the feast days holy.
3. My friends will be Jesus and Mary.
4. Death, rather than sin.

St. John Bosco, his mentor and teacher said, "These resolutions, which he often repeated, governed his conduct to the end of his life."

> *We need to lose our fear before that presence which can only be for our good. God is the Father who gave us life and loves us greatly. Once we accept him, and stop trying to live our lives without him, the anguish of loneliness will appear (cf. Psalm 139:23–24).*
>
> —Pope Francis, Gaudete Et Exsultate, 51

> *But you must fear the LORD and serve him faithfully with all your heart, for you have seen the great things the LORD has done among you.*
> — Samuel 12:24

> *The beginning of wisdom is fear of the LORD.*
> —Proverbs 9:10

> *Let all the earth fear the LORD; Let all the inhabitants of the world stand in awe of Him.*
> —Psalm 33:8

> *His mercy is from age to age to those who fear him.*
> —Luke 1:50

HOPE

PRAY IT *LECTIO DIVINA*

Luke 12:16–34

Then he told them a parable. "There was a rich man whose land produced a bountiful harvest. He asked himself, 'What shall I do, for I do not have space to store my harvest?' And he said, 'This is what I shall do: I shall tear down my barns and build larger ones. There I shall store all my grain and other goods and I shall say to myself, "Now as for you, you have so many good things stored up for many years, rest, eat, drink, be merry!"' But God said to him, 'You fool, this night your life will be demanded of you; and the things you have prepared, to whom will they belong?' Thus will it be for the one who stores up treasure for himself but is not rich in what matters to God." He said to [his] disciples, "Therefore I tell you, do not worry about your life and what you will eat, or about your body and what you will wear. For life is more than food and the body more than clothing. Notice the ravens: they do not sow or reap; they have neither storehouse nor barn, yet God feeds them. How much more important are you than birds! Can any of you by worrying add a moment to your life-span? If even the smallest things are beyond your control, why are you anxious about the rest? Notice how the flowers grow. They do not toil or spin. But I tell you, not even Solomon in all his splendor was dressed like one of them. If God so clothes the grass in the field that grows today and is thrown into the oven tomorrow, will he not much more provide for you, O you of little faith? As for you, do not seek what you are to eat and what you are to drink, and do not worry anymore. All the nations of the world seek for these things, and your Father knows that you need them. Instead, seek his kingdom, and these other things will be given you besides. Do not be afraid any longer, little flock, for your Father is pleased to give you the kingdom. Sell your belongings and give alms. Provide money bags for yourselves that do not wear out, an inexhaustible treasure in heaven that no thief can reach nor moth destroy. For where your treasure is, there also will your heart be."

1. God's Word strikes the heart. What word or phrase touched your heart?
2. How was the rich man foolish? What are the "riches" that matter to God?
3. Select two examples of how we can be assured of God's providential care for us.
4. Read verses 21 ("Thus will it be…") and 34 (the last verse). Think about the treasures in your life. Is your heart properly ordered?
5. Ask this question in prayer: "Jesus, You have revealed to us how God the Father provides for His creation. In what ways does He care for me and my life?" Write down what He reveals to you.

PRAY IT

Pray an Act of Hope

O Lord God,

I hope by Your grace for the pardon of all my sins and after life here to gain eternal happiness, because You have promised it, Who are infinitely powerful, faithful, kind, and merciful. In this hope I intend to live and die. Amen.

When our heart is anchored in God, we have confidence in His divine providence and seek to store up treasure in heaven. The theological virtue of hope enables one to desire God above all things and to trust Him for personal salvation.

HOPE

LIVE IT — LOOKING TO THE SAINTS

ST. JOSEPHINE BAKHITA

Josephine Bakhita was born around 1869 in Sudan. We know next to nothing about Josephine's early life because her earliest memories were blocked by the overwhelming trauma of her young life.

When she was nine, Josephine was kidnapped by Arab slave traders. The experience was so horrifying that the young girl forgot her name. Her captors called her "Bakhita," which means "lucky." Over the next twelve years, she experienced cruel treatment at the hands of various masters. In the home of a Turkish general, the mistress had designs carved into the flesh of her slaves. Then, to make sure the scars would be permanent, salt was rubbed into the wounds. Josephine bore 114 scars across her body.

> **Abiding with Hope**
>
> She came to know that this Lord even knew her, that He had created her—that He actually loved her."

At the age of fourteen, Josephine was sold again to an Italian consul who was different than any other master she had known. For the first time, she experienced kindness, even affection. She was learning the Venetian dialect and called her master "paron." In the kindness of this home, she came to know the love of the supreme Paron. She found in Jesus "a paron above all masters, the Lord of all lords, and that this Lord is goodness in person. She came to know that this Lord even knew her, that He had created her—that He actually loved her" (*Spes Salvi*, 3). In this new reality, Josephine was redeemed, a free daughter of God. Her whole outlook on life changed.

Josephine had the option to stay in Sudan or go to Italy. She chose Italy, knowing that she would be able to enter the Church there. On January 9, 1890 she was baptized with the name "Josephine." Six years later she made vows as a Canossian Sister in Verona. She was an impassioned advocate for the missions knowing firsthand what it is like to move from death to life.

Hope gives an assurance that is rooted in Christ Jesus. Pope Benedict said it this way: "I am definitely loved and whatever happens to me—I am awaited by this Love. And so my life is good." (*Spes Salvi*, 3). When people marveled at the serenity of Sr. Josephine as she shared her testimony, they were marveling at the fruit of a life of hope.

LIVE IT

HOPE

HOPE enables one to desire God above all things and to trust Him for personal salvation.

A Disciple of Christ living the virtue of hope...

Knows that heaven is our true home

Strives to live the Beatitudes

Accepts sufferings and trials with patience, perseverance, and even joy

Nourishes and expresses it in prayer

Finds comfort in the recollection of God's love, shown to us to by Christ's death on the Cross

Looks to the saints as friends, intercessors, and guides along the journey to heaven

In the Words of Pope Francis...

Do not be afraid of holiness. It will take away none of your energy, vitality or joy. On the contrary, you will become what the Father had in mind when he created you, and you will be faithful to your deepest self. To depend on God sets us free from every form of enslavement and leads us to recognize our great dignity. We see this in Saint Josephine Bakhita: "Abducted and sold into slavery at the tender age of seven, she suffered much at the hands of cruel masters. But she came to understand the profound truth that God, and not man, is the true Master of every human being, of every human life. This experience became a source of great wisdom for this humble daughter of Africa."

—Pope Francis, Gaudete Et Exsultate, 32

Going Deeper in Hope

FROM THE CATECHISM

Hope is the theological virtue by which we desire the kingdom of heaven and eternal life as our happiness, placing our trust in Christ's promises and relying not on our own strength but on the help of the grace of the Holy Spirit. "Let us hold fast the confession of our hope without wavering, for he who promised is faithful" (Hebrews 10:23). "The Holy Spirit…he poured out upon us richly through Jesus Christ our Savior, so that we might be justified by his grace and become heirs in hope of eternal life" [Titus 3:6–7] (*CCC*, 1817).

■ **Hope** gives youthful freedom because one lives in expectation of eternal beatitude (heaven).

We see as a distinguishing mark of Christians the fact that they have a future: it is not that they know the details of what awaits them, but they know in general terms that their life will not end in emptiness. Only when the future is certain as a positive reality does it become possible to live the present as well. So now we can say: Christianity was not only "good news"—the communication of a hitherto unknown content. In our language we would say: the Christian message was not only "informative" but "performative." That means: the Gospel is not merely a communication of things that can be known—it is one that makes things happen and is life-changing. The dark door of time, of the future, has been thrown open. The one who has hope lives differently; the one who hopes has been granted the gift of a new life (Pope Benedict XVI, *Spe Salvi*, 2; see also *CCC*, 1818).

■ **Hope** anchors the soul in God and enables one to be joyful under trial.

Christian hope unfolds from the beginning of Jesus' preaching in the proclamation of the beatitudes. The beatitudes raise our hope toward heaven as the new Promised Land; they trace the path that leads through the trials that await the disciples of Jesus. But through the merits of Jesus Christ and of his Passion, God keeps us in the "hope that does not disappoint" (Romans 5:5).

> Hope is the "sure and steadfast anchor of the soul … that enters … where Jesus has gone as a forerunner on our behalf" (Hebrews 6:19–20).
>
> Hope is also a weapon that protects us in the struggle of salvation: "Let us… put on the breastplate of faith and charity, and for a helmet the hope of salvation" (1 Thessalonians 5:8).
>
> Hope affords us joy even under trial: "Rejoice in your hope, be patient in tribulation" (Romans 12:12).
>
> Hope is expressed and nourished in prayer, especially in the Our Father, the summary of everything that hope leads us to desire (*CCC*, 1820; cf. 1716, 2772).

Going Deeper in Hope

Despair is the intellectual and willful rejection of God's forgiveness and heaven as our final end. Two vices which frequently cause despair are **acedia** (spiritual sloth) and **unchastity**.

- **Acedia** (spiritual sloth) is one of the capital sins and manifests itself in various ways. It is important to educate oneself in these manifestations in order to guard oneself from this vice.
- Sins of **unchastity** cause a lack of the integration of sexuality within a person and thus a lack of unity between man's bodily and spiritual being (cf. *CCC*, 2351–2356, 2380).

ACEDIA (SPIRITUAL SLOTH)
is a form of depression caused by neglecting the faith and moral life.

MANIFESTATIONS OF ACEDIA

Uneasy restlessness of the mind	Apathy with regard to everything man needs for salvation	"Small soul"; faintheartedness; lacking courage to pursue the spiritual life	Nursing grudges	Spitefulness	
EVAGATIO MENTIS	TORPOR	PUSILLANIMITY	RANCOR	MALICE	DESPAIR
EVAGATIO MENTIS, TORPOR, PUSILLANIMITY, RANCOR, MALICE					DESPAIR
REJECTIONS OF THE MEANS TO THE END					**REJECTION OF THE END (HEAVEN)**

Shows itself by:

- Loquaciousness, talkativeness
- Excessive curiosity
- Instability of place or of purpose
- Restlessness of the body; exterior manifestations of interior unrest and wandering of the mind
- Disorder of the mind; mind goes from one thing to another in a way that suits only its own needs and desires, not according to reason

Going Deeper in Hope

Acedia and the Third Commandment

By the Third Commandment, we must worship God. God commands us to worship Him, not for His sake, but for ours. We are made holy (and whole) when we are in right relationship with God. Sunday is not only a day of worship, it is also a day of rest for the rejuvenation of man's spiritual and physical powers. Acedia robs man of the ability to worship and to rest. Acedia, by attacking our relationship with God, the interior order that is restored by a life of virtue is unable to be achieved.

By contrast, the link between the Lord's Day and the day of rest in civil society has a meaning and importance which go beyond the distinctly Christian point of view. The alternation between work and rest, built into human nature, is willed by God himself, as appears in the creation story in the Book of Genesis (cf. 2:2–3; Exodus 20:8–11): rest is something "sacred," because it is man's way of withdrawing from the sometimes excessively demanding cycle of earthly tasks in order to renew his awareness that everything is the work of God. There is a risk that the prodigious power over creation which God gives to man can lead him to forget that God is the Creator upon whom everything depends (St. Pope John Paul II, Dies Domini, *65).*

When, during the persecution of Diocletian, their assemblies were banned with the greatest severity, many were courageous enough to defy the imperial decree and accepted death rather than miss the Sunday Eucharist. This was the case of the martyrs of Abitina, in Proconsular Africa, who replied to their accusers: "Without fear of any kind we have celebrated the Lord's Supper, because it cannot be missed; that is our law"; "we cannot live without the Lord's Supper" (St. Pope John Paul II, Dies Domini, *46).*

The Blessed Virgin Mary and the Gifts of the Holy Spirit

The Annunciation to Mary and the Gift of Fear of the Lord

We pray and we hope that our prayers will be heard and answered. But what would we ever do if that answer took the form of a radiant angel speaking our name in the middle of our living room? It would probably terrify us just as it apparently terrified Mary. Gabriel soothes her with the words, "Do not fear, Mary" (Luke 1:30). The archangel frees Mary from her fright so as to bless her with the holy Fear of the Lord. For the Holy Spirit's Gift of Fear disposes us to reverence God and to be completely devoted to him. Sanctified Fear of the Lord enables the Blessed Mother to show God the same devotion that he shows to her: "O highly favored daughter! The Lord is with you. Blessed are you among women" (Luke 1:28).

Fear of the Lord strengthens, renews, and refashions Mary's hope. In response to the angel's revelations, the Blessed Mother asks: "How can this be?" In the answer Gabriel gives, powerful hope is also given as well. Fear of the Lord helps Mary—and us—to see beyond whatever we consider constraining, unlikely, or impossible in our life. It opens up for us the boundlessness of God's mercy and providence. All the Lord asks of us to do in response is to rely utterly on his divine help. Fear of the Lord prevents us from ever disregarding God's assistance. Holy fear reminds us how crucial and urgent God's interaction in our life must remain in order for us to be happy, holy, and hope-filled.

At the same time, we see in Mary how "fear of the Lord is the beginning of wisdom" (Psalm 111:10). For in reverencing and believing the excellence of God revealed in the archangel Gabriel, the Blessed Mother manifests the right judgment she has about divine things. Her grace as Seat of Wisdom has begun to function in the reverent fear in which she receives God's messenger and accepts his message of Wisdom Incarnate.

Through this transforming experience of sanctified fear, Mary is called to look upon God in a new way. The angel announces that God is now her Spouse. St. Louis de Montfort writes: "The Holy Spirit became fruitful through Mary whom he espoused. To his faithful spouse, Mary, the Holy Spirit has communicated his ineffable gifts, and he has chosen her to dispense all that he possesses. The Holy Spirit says to Mary: 'You are still My Spouse, unswervingly faithful, pure, and fruitful.'"

And what is Mary's response to all this? The profound humility that is Fear's effect. "Mary said, 'I am the servant of the Lord. Let it be done to me as you say'" (Luke 1:38). She gives herself to God as a servant…but not in a servile manner. Her concern is only to love God more, to fulfill his will, to avoid whatever might offend him, and to grow closer to him in love and devotion. In her utter poverty and humility, the Blessed Mother seeks nothing for herself. "Full of grace," Mary's Immaculate Heart is so absolutely disinclined to sin that Fear of the Lord prompts her to shun all evil as she awaits the birth of the Savior in perfect tranquility. And as we remain united to the Blessed Mother in her Fear of the Lord, her confidence and tranquility become our own. As Mary's life and song proclaim: "God's mercy is from age to age on those who fear him" (Luke 1:50).

"The Annunciation to Mary and the Gift of the Fear of the Lord," pg. 31. Cameron, Peter John O.P. *The Gifts of the Holy Spirit*. Veritas Series. Connecticut: Knights of Columbus, 2002.

BURNING WITH CHARITY

CHARITY

Charity, usually represented by a heart, enables one to love as God Himself loves. By this virtue we love God above all things and are more concerned about our neighbor than we are about ourselves.

Love is often represented by a heart. Charity, since it is God's own love, is best represented by the Sacred Heart of Jesus. The heart is our hidden center, the place of decision, the place where we encounter God.

Jesus Christ took upon Himself our humanity; now He loves us with a divine and human love. Jesus shows us how to love. Like the burning bush on Mt. Sinai, God's love sets our human hearts on fire, but it will never destroy us. Love is willing to sacrifice for the beloved, just as Jesus was crowned with thorns and died on the cross for our salvation.

In this is love: not that we have loved God, but that he loved us and sent his Son as expiation for our sins."

—1 John 4:10

CHARITY

KNOW IT

CHARITY enables one to love as God Himself loves, to love God above all things and one's neighbor as oneself.

Charity is the theological virtue given to us at Baptism. It is a supernatural gift given to us by God so that we, who are loved by God, are able to love God in a free gift of self. It imparts spiritual freedom, the freedom of a child confident in the Father's love for His children. It is not motivated by fear or a desire for reward. Rather, it is the response to the free gift of God's love. Charity enables the Christian to love and accept others as freely and unconditionally as he loves himself.

The practice of all the virtues is animated and inspired by charity, which "binds everything together in perfect harmony" [Colossians 3:14]; it is the *form of the virtues;* it articulates and orders them among themselves; it is the source and the goal of their Christian practice. Charity upholds and purifies our human ability to love, and raises it to the supernatural perfection of divine love (*CCC,* 1827).

Theological Virtue of Charity

CCC, 1822–1829

CCC, 1844

Sins Against Charity

CCC, 2094

Summa Theologiae

II–II.Q23–24, St. Thomas Aquinas

Echoing the Mystery

43-Love

Key Points

- Charity is a supernatural gift of God infused at Baptism.
- Charity is the form that binds all the virtue together.
- Charity is the proper order of love—love of God, love of self, love of neighbor.

GUARD IT

CHARITY

The theological virtue of charity enables one to love as God loves. It sanctifies the human heart, enabling him to will the good of the other. In order to guard our charity, we must learn to love God above all things. As we learn to see ourselves in God, we will be able to have a proper self-love and thus love others as we love ourselves.

Some of the ways we can sin against charity include the following:

Hatred of God	Prideful rejection of God and God's love; cursing God as One who forbids sins and punishes man's disobedience
Hatred toward neighbor	Willfully wishing harm to one's neighbor (see also *CCC*, 2303)
Acedia	A capital vice that goes so far as to sustain a state of dejection in the face of goodness (see acedia chart page 40)
Ingratitude	Failing to properly acknowledge God's goodness and love
Indifference	Neglecting or simply not caring about God's love
Lukewarmness	A halfhearted response to God's love, lacking conviction
Envy	Sadness at the sight of another's goods and the immoderate desire to acquire them for oneself, even unjustly; a mortal sin when it wishes grave harm to a neighbor
Discord	Conflict of wills arising from pride, clinging inordinately to one's will, and despising the opinions of others
Contention	Bickering, unreasonable arguing, clinging to one's own way and opinion, arguing stubbornly, even in the face of contrary evidence and manifestation of the truth

> "If God is love, charity should know no limit, for God cannot be confined."
> —St. Leo the Great

> "Charity for the poor is like a living flame, the drier the fuel, the brighter it burns. In your service to the poor do not give only your hands but also your hearts. To love, it is necessary to give: to give it is necessary to be free from selfishness."
> —St. Teresa of Calcutta, *Mother Teresa, Her Essential Wisdom*

> St. Augustine saw envy as "the diabolical sin." "From envy are born hatred, detraction, calumny, joy caused by the misfortune of a neighbor, and displeasure caused by his prosperity."
> —*CCC*, 2539, quoting St. Augustine, *De catechizandis rudibus*, 4, 8; St. Gregory the Great, *Moralia in Job*, 31, 45

> So faith, hope, love remain, these three; but the greatest of these is love.
> —1 Corinthians 13:13

CHARITY

KNOW IT

RELATED BEATITUDE

The Gift of Wisdom

"Blessed are the peacemakers, for they shall be called sons and daughters of God." —Matthew 5:9

A peacemaker is one who is at peace in himself and in others. Peace extends beyond the absence of conflict to the tranquility of right order. Therefore, a peacemaker strives to live in harmony with God seeking to order all things, according to His divine providence.

Summa Theologiae

II–II.Q45–46, St. Thomas Aquinas

WISDOM moves one to order one's life according to God's will.

The theological virtue of charity gives us a sharing in God's own love, enabling us to love as He loves. There arises in any relationship, a sort of connatural or shared knowledge between people who love each other. By the **Gift of Wisdom**, God shares with us His own knowledge; we see God's plan of the world from within. We now see things from God's perspective, able to grasp the whole and penetrate to the heart of the matter. From this new perspective, we are able to judge rightly all things in light of eternal wisdom and share in His joy.

Effects of the Gift of the Holy Spirit

- Delights in spiritual things; experiences the sweetness of God
- Sees God in every aspect of creation
- Judges things and actions according to eternal wisdom
- Focuses on what truly matters, able to set priorities
- Devotes time to daily prayer and the sacramental life

GUARD IT

- **Folly:** We need to guard our ways of thinking and acting. The sin of folly impedes our openness to the Spirit of the gift of wisdom. Folly denotes a loss of true judgment, when someone is unable to see the true value of things, or even of life itself. The foolish person is willing to exchange spiritual goods (such as personal integrity or friendship with God) for a passing worldly good (such as pleasure, honor, or wealth). Folly, or this dullness in judgment, often arises from gluttony and lust.

PRAY IT *LECTIO DIVINA*

John 4:7–12

Beloved, let us love one another, because love is of God; everyone who loves is begotten by God and knows God. Whoever is without love does not know God, for God is love. In this way the love of God was revealed to us: God sent his only Son into the world so that we might have life through him. In this is love: not that we have loved God, but that he loved us and sent his Son as expiation for our sins. Beloved, if God so loved us, we also must love one another. No one has ever seen God. Yet, if we love one another, God remains in us, and his love is brought to perfection in us.

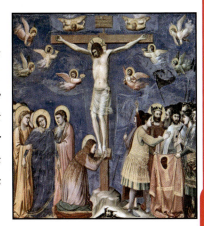

1. God's Word strikes the heart. What word or phrase touched your heart?
2. God first loved us. How does this impact your life and view of God?
3. How will this knowledge that God loved you first sustain you in difficult situations?
4. The proper order of love is love of God, love of self, love of neighbor. How does this enable you to love others?
5. What are some concrete ways to show your love of God and neighbor?
6. Ask this question in prayer: "Jesus, how can I be a witness of Your love to others?" Write down what He says to you.

Pray an Act of Charity

O My God,

I love You above all things with my whole heart and soul because You are all good and worthy of all my love. I love my neighbor as myself for the love of You. I forgive all who have injured me and ask pardon of all whom I have injured. Amen.

CHARITY

LIVE IT — LOOKING TO THE SAINTS

ST. TERESA OF CALCUTTA

Gonxha (Agnes) Bojaxhiu was born on August 27, 1910, the youngest in her family. Her father was a contractor and died suddenly when Gonxha was seven years old. As a child she was fascinated by stories of missionaries, inspired by their sacrifice and service. She entered the Loreto Sisters when she was eighteen, moving to Ireland to begin her novitiate.

The following year the young sister was sent to Darjeeling, India. She took the name Teresa, after St. Thérèse of Lisieux, inspired by the Little Flower's mission to love. She was assigned to teach in a girls' high school in Calcutta, where, for the next fifteen years, she taught history and geography. The school was in a protected environment, a little haven of comfort surrounded by the abject poverty of the streets of Calcutta. Her students loved her, and she loved them. But her heart went out to the poor, and she helped the young women learn to see the dignity and worth of each poor person.

> **Burning with Charity**
>
> "Not all of us can do great things, but we can do small things with great love."

In 1946, while on a train to Darjeeling for a retreat, she heard what she later described as a "call within a call." God was asking her to leave the security of Loreto to serve the poorest of the poor—the destitute, the dying—on the streets of Calcutta. There was no one else to love them, so she would.

She received permission to leave the Loreto convent and go out to the streets. With alarming simplicity, she began with no clear plan or provisions. She began teaching the poorest children in the slums, gathering them around her and using the ground as her chalkboard. She visited the poor and the sick in their shacks and eased the last days of the dying. She chose a simple white sari with a blue border for her habit. Soon, young women began to join her, most of them her former students. By 1950, she received approval for a new religious congregation: Missionaries of Charity.

For the next forty-seven years, Mother Teresa loved and served the poorest of the poor. Like her patron, St. Thérèse, she taught that love was not primarily about grand actions. "Not all of us can do great things," she said, "but we can do small things with great love." She saw that spiritual poverty was rampant in the world. Feeling unloved, unwanted, forgotten by everyone was a worst poverty than the poverty of food or clothing. That was the poverty that only love could fill.

Mother Teresa's love for others cannot be understood apart from her deep faith in Jesus Christ. "I believe that God loves the world through us—through you and me." Her love of Christ in the Eucharist opened her eyes to see and love Christ in the poor. She took to heart the passage about the sheep and the goats, where the Lord says, "whatever you did for one of these least brothers of mine, you did for me" (Matthew 25:40). She fed the hungry, clothed the naked, gave drink to the thirsty, visited the sick, and buried the dead because of her love for Jesus. Jesus allowed Mother Teresa to share in His thirst on the Cross. Mother Teresa daily chose love, proclaiming by the witness of her life the power of unconditional love.

LIVE IT

CHARITY

CHARITY enables one to love as God Himself loves, to love God above all things and one's neighbor as oneself.

A Disciple of Christ living the virtue of charity…

Spiritual Works of Mercy

- ✓ Teaches the Ignorant
- ✓ Counsels the Doubtful
- ✓ Admonishes the Sinner
- ✓ Bears Wrongs Patiently
- ✓ Forgives Offenses
- ✓ Comforts the Sorrowful
- ✓ Prays For the Living and the Dead

Corporal Works of Mercy

- ✓ Gives Food to the Hungry
- ✓ Gives Drink to the Thirsty
- ✓ Clothes the Naked
- ✓ Shelters the Homeless
- ✓ Visits the Sick
- ✓ Visits the Imprisoned
- ✓ Buries the Dead

In the Words of St. Pope John Paul II…

As disciples of Jesus, we are called to become neighbors to everyone (cf. Luke 10:29–37), and to show special favor to those who are poorest, most alone, and most in need. In helping the hungry, the thirsty, the foreigner, the naked, the sick, the imprisoned—as well as the child in the womb and the old person who is suffering or near death—we have the opportunity to serve Jesus. —St. Pope John Paul II, General Audience, Wednesday, 27 September 1978

Going Deeper in Charity

FROM THE CATECHISM

By charity, we love God above all things and our neighbor as ourselves for love of God. Charity, the form of all the virtues, "binds everything together in perfect harmony" [Colossians 3:14] (*CCC*, 1844).

The practice of the moral life animated by charity gives to the Christian the spiritual freedom of the children of God. He no longer stands before God as a slave, in servile fear, or as a mercenary looking for wages, but as a son responding to the love of him who "first loved us" [see 1 John 4:19]:

If we turn away from evil out of fear of punishment, we are in the position of slaves. If we pursue the enticement of wages...we resemble mercenaries. Finally if we obey for the sake of the good itself and out of love for him who commands...we are in the position of children (*CCC*, 1828, quoting St. Basil, *Greater Monastic Rules*).

Fruits of Charity

"Children, let us love not in word or speech, but in deed and truth" (John 3:18). Charity manifests itself in the following fruits:

■ **Internal Fruits of Charity**
- Joy: Effect of charity whereby one delights in the goodness of God
- Peace: Interior harmony in all the desires and tendencies of one's heart
- Mercy: Loving-kindness, especially toward one who offends

■ **External Fruits of Charity**
- Beneficence (kindness): doing good to or for another
- Almsgiving: giving to the needy out of compassion and for the sake of God
- Fraternal Correction: prayerfully, prudently, and lovingly leading another toward the greater good

The Blessed Virgin Mary and the Gifts of the Holy Spirit

The Passion, Pentecost, and the Gift of Wisdom

"Near the cross of Jesus there stood his mother" (John 19:25). How could Mary endure to witness the agony of her Son? Wisdom empowered her to witness this Passion. For Mary's Son is not just any Son; he is the Word—not just any word, but the Word breathing love. St. Thomas Aquinas wrote that "the Son's being sent is that sort of enlightening that bursts forth in love." Even in the midst of his excruciating death, Jesus offers anyone who looks upon him with love a special knowledge and perception of himself. In his Passion—especially in the Eucharist—Jesus offers us a knowing that we can taste. This is Wisdom. This is the knowledge the Blessed Mother experiences on Calvary even as she shares in the agony of her Son. The wise person is one who considers the ultimate cause of things and uses it to judge other things with certainty.

The wise person's attention to the ultimate cause of things gives him or her a standard to set all things in order. The Spirit's Gift of Wisdom enables us to judge and to set in order everything in our life according to God's rules. Despite the suffering of the Passion, this Gift enabled the Blessed Mother to see beyond the anguish to the ultimate cause and the ultimate need for her Son to die for sinners. That experiential awareness equipped Mary to make the right judgment about what was happening on Golgotha. It gave her the confidence to regard the event according to God's rules and to trust that, even in the chaos of crucifixion, divine providence was maintaining everything in right order.

The Gift of Wisdom judges all things according to divine truth. Mary's faith-filled wisdom leads her to regard the horrible tragedy of the Passion solely according to God's truth. The same applies to us. Through the Gift of Wisdom, we rely confidently on divine truth to make sense of all the absurdity, the sorrow, the heartbreak, and the calamity in our life. Even amidst catastrophe and disaster, Wisdom restores order and divine purpose to our life. It gives us confidence that every fractured piece of our life is made whole as it finds its rightful place in the merciful plan of God's Providence. If we have the grace to accept God's rules, God's rules will reign in our pain.

Wisdom also is at work with the Apostles and the Blessed Mother in the Upper Room on Pentecost (see also Acts 1:13–14). For it belongs to Wisdom first to contemplate divine realities, and then to direct human action according to divine reasons. Together they contemplate the outpouring of the Holy Spirit with all his Gifts. And by the divine Wisdom they share, they direct others through evangelization to follow the Way who is Jesus. They bring about peace by putting "first things first" in the tranquility of order through the power of the Gift of Wisdom. They lead others to embrace the Wisdom of divine reasoning, and thereby to enter into the state of being children of God. And Mary, the Mother of God's Son, is also our Mother as Wisdom begets us as children of the Father. For, in his infinite wisdom and love, Jesus gives us Mary to be our Mother as his final gift to us from the Cross.

"The Passion, Pentecost and the Gift of Wisdom," pg. 40. Cameron, Peter John O.P. *The Gifts of the Holy Spirit*. Veritas Series. Connecticut: Knights of Columbus, 2002.

ACTING
WITH PRUDENCE

PRUDENCE

Prudence can be represented by a scroll and torch. Prudence is right reason in action. Illumined by the light of faith, Christian prudence is able to see clearly even in the midst of darkness to know the truth and the best way to act in any situation.

"The lamp of the body is the eye. If your eye is sound, your whole body will be filled with light; but if your eye is bad, your whole body will be in darkness. And if the light in you is darkness, how great will the darkness be."

—Matthew 6:22-23

RELATED VIRTUES:

CIRCUMSPECTION   DOCILITY   FORESIGHT

PRUDENCE

KNOW IT

> **PRUDENCE** enables one to reason and to act rightly in any given situation — "right reason in action."

Prudence is the cardinal virtue that perfects our intellect, our natural ability to judge correctly. More simply, prudence perfects our common sense. It guides the other virtues because by setting the standard and measure. When illumined by faith, Christian prudence enables us to judge situations in light of eternity. In helping us make good decisions, prudence applies moral principles to specific cases. Its decisions are clear, so that we are able to overcome doubts about the good we desire to achieve and the evil we wish to avoid. In practicing prudence, the Christian is able to do "whatever is true, whatever is honorable, whatever is just, whatever is pure, whatever is lovely, whatever is gracious" (Philippians 4:8).

Cardinal Virtue of Prudence

CCC, 1786–1789
CCC, 1806
CCC, 1835

Summa Theologiae

II–II.Q47–56, St. Thomas Aquinas

Echoing the Mystery

48–Cardinal Virtue of Prudence

Three Parts of a Prudential Act:

There are three parts in the decision-making process. The virtue of prudence orders and perfects each of the following:

PARTS OF A PRUDENTIAL ACT		OPPOSING TRAIT
GOOD COUNSEL	Seeking advice from reasonable and trustworthy persons	Seeking advice from those who agree with you or do not share your moral values
GOOD JUDGMENT	Thinking rightly about a decision, carefully considering all the circumstances, and praying about what the Lord would have you do	Acting without thinking
COMMAND	Acting upon a sound decision made after thoughtful deliberation	Failing to act upon a sound decision

1. Ask and Listen
2. Think
3. Act

Key Points

- Aims to perfect one's natural ability to judge, one's common sense
- Guides one in making good moral choices

PRUDENCE

GUARD IT

ACTING WITH PRUDENCE

The cardinal virtue of prudence aims to perfect our common sense in both practical and moral decisions. It is right reason in action. At our Baptism, our heavenly Father gave us this virtue to aid us in making good decisions. Like any gift, it must be guarded from that which prevents us from cultivating good habits.

Integral Parts of Prudence:

Prudence, because it guides our decision making, influences every aspect of our life. It is a fundamental virtue in human life. As such, it has several key elements. When we actively engage the various parts of prudence in making decisions, we guard the virtue of prudence by avoiding the sins that endanger it.

1. **Memory**: The recollection of previous events and what one has learned from them.
2. **Understanding**: The ability to grasp situations and know what to do.
3. **Docility**: The willingness to be taught and open to advice of others, especially from those who know more.
4. **Shrewdness**: The ability to determine quickly what is best in a situation.
5. **Reason**: The proper use of one's mind in making a decision.
6. **Foresight**: The ability to think ahead and consider possible consequences.
7. **Circumspection**: The ability to look around and consider the impact on others.
8. **Precaution**: The ability to consider possible obstacles, including one's inabilities.

Sins against prudence include the following:

Imprudence		
Impulsivity	Acting without thinking, hastily	Impedes good counsel
Inconsideration	Not wanting to make a decision or ignoring necessary information for making a right judgment	Impedes good judgment
Inconstancy/ procrastination	Lack of resolve, giving up, not following through on a decision	Impedes command
Negligence	Lack of interest in pursuing counsel or sound judgment	

> *Prudence is a bold virtue. It sees the bearing of conduct, not upon our immediate convenience, but upon our ultimate salvation.*
>
> —Frank Sheed, Theology and Sanity

> *The person who has sacrificed much in order to follow the supernatural goals set by our Lord Jesus Christ may look unfortunate in the eyes of the world, but he or she will have greater interior peace. That alone makes supernatural prudence the wisest and most acceptable way to walk in this confusing world.*
>
> —Fr. Benedict Groeschel, The Virtue Driven Life

> *Prudence means searching for the truth and acting, in conformity with it. The prudent servant is first and foremost a man of truth and a man of sincere reason.*
>
> —Pope Benedict XVI, Homily, September 11, 2009

> *The truthful witness saves lives, but whoever utters lies is a betrayer.*
>
> —Proverbs 14:25

PRUDENCE

KNOW IT

RELATED BEATITUDE

The Gift of Counsel

"Blessed are the merciful, for they shall obtain mercy."
—Matthew 5:7

The Gift of Counsel leads one to pardon others because God sees humanity with the eyes of mercy, and He opens man's heart to treat others with mercy in turn.

Summa Theologiae

II–II.Q52, St. Thomas Aquinas

COUNSEL enables one to respond fully to direction and guidance from the Lord.

The cardinal virtue of prudence perfects our intellect, enabling us to act rightly in any given situation. The gifts of knowledge, understanding, and wisdom all deal with the things of God. In the **Gift of Counsel** the Holy Spirit aids us in the practical application of spiritual truths in our daily lives. It can be likened to prudence for spiritual realities, able to discern what is good for our spiritual life and act on that decision. Because the virtuous disciple has a familiarity with the workings of God, he is easily able to make choices that are in accordance with His will.

Effects of the Gift of the Holy Spirit

- Judges correctly the means on the way toward our heavenly homeland
- Discerns easily and act on moral decisions
- Imparts confidence, peace, and joy, especially in regards to one's decisions
- Trusts the good advice from spiritual guides
- Gives good advice, maintaining the dignity of the person
- Shows mercy and kindness to others
- Maintains the docile stance of a disciple, always ready to learn from the Church

PRUDENCE

PRAY IT *LECTIO DIVINA*

Matthew 25:1–13

"Then the kingdom of heaven will be like ten virgins who took their lamps and went out to meet the bridegroom. Five of them were foolish and five were wise. The foolish ones, when taking their lamps, brought no oil with them, but the wise brought flasks of oil with their lamps. Since the bridegroom was long delayed, they all became drowsy and fell asleep. At midnight, there was a cry, 'Behold, the bridegroom! Come out to meet him!' Then all those virgins got up and trimmed their lamps. The foolish ones said to the wise, 'Give us some of your oil, for our lamps are going out.' But the wise ones replied, 'No, for there may not be enough for us and you. Go instead to the merchants and buy some for yourselves.' While they went off to buy it, the bridegroom came and those who were ready went into the wedding feast with him. Then the door was locked. Afterwards the other virgins came and said, 'Lord, Lord, open the door for us!' But he said in reply, 'Amen, I say to you, I do not know you.' Therefore, stay awake, for you know neither the day nor the hour."

1. God's Word strikes the heart. What word or phrase touched your heart?
2. Describe the words and actions of the foolish virgins.
3. Describe the words and actions of the wise virgins.
4. The wise virgins' lamps were filled with oil which symbolized how their lives were spent in prayer and acts of love. Why couldn't this be shared with the foolish virgins?
5. Ask this question in prayer: "Jesus, Bridegroom, You call all of us to the kingdom of heaven, and yet the oil of our hearts must always be burning. Show me how I should live to always have my lamp filled with oil." Write down what He says to you.

Pray an Act of Prudence

Dear Jesus,

In my thoughts, words, and actions I can give You praise. Always grant me the grace to know the truth, to speak always what is right, and to follow You in all I do.

PRUDENCE

LIVE IT — LOOKING TO THE SAINTS

BL. STANLEY ROTHER

Stanley was born on an Oklahoma farm on March 27, 1935. He was the oldest of four children and went to the local parish school. He grew up working the farm, getting up early to do chores before school and participated in sports in the afternoon. He wasn't the smartest kid in school, but he was good with his hands and was always willing to help someone else. He went to the seminary after high school. But at seminary Stanley struggled with his classes, especially Latin. The seminary told his bishop that they did not think Stanley was cut out to be a priest since he could not pass Latin.

> **Acting with Prudence**
>
> He told his brother that "a shepherd cannot run from his flock."

When Stanley was back home, he had long conversations with his bishop about what to do. He was open about his academic struggles, but also about his sincere desire to serve the People of God as a priest. The bishop was supportive and worked with Mount Saint Mary's Seminary in Emmitsburg, Maryland to find a place for Stanley. Throughout his time at the Mount, Stanley regularly went to the grotto to think and pray, asking for the Lord's guidance in his life. He was ordained in 1963.

In 1968, Father Stanley requested permission to serve at his diocese's mission in Santiago Atitlan, Guatemala. He flourished in the mission. All his natural talents of farming, building, and mechanics were put to good use helping the Tz'utujil people. The seminarian who struggled with Latin learned Tz'utujil so he could preach in the people's native language. He was unafraid of manual labor, and this quickly won him the esteem of the people. He visited them in their homes, sitting on the dirt floors and sharing their simple meals with them.

A civil war between the militarist government and guerrilla groups was soon raging in Guatemala. Both sides would have liked to claim the support of the Catholic Church, and there were many priests in Latin America who sided with left-winged guerrillas against the oppressive regime. When the violence came closer to the remote village, Father Stan reinforced the locks on the church and rectory, avoided going out at night, even slept with his shoes on. He kept his bishop back in Oklahoma updated on the situation. He was no political activist and was not influenced by the liberation theology that appealed to so many other priests. Nevertheless, he would not stop caring for his people, especially the widows and orphans of men who were kidnapped and killed by the army.

In January 1981, Father Stan received a tip that he was a marked man. He hid in Guatemala City until he was able to fly to the United States. He and his bishop again had long conversations, both aware of the danger to Father Stan's life if he went back to Guatemala. While on retreat back at the Mount, he again spent time in prayer in chapel and in the grotto. Then he told his brother that "a shepherd cannot run from his flock," and returned Santiago Atitlan in time for Holy Week.

On July 28, 1981, three men broke into Father Stanley's rectory in the middle of the night. A fight ensued as Father Stan tried to defend himself, but he was shot dead. The Tz'utujil were shocked, and, as they assembled in the churchyard, there was a murmur, "they killed our priest." It could have easily turned into a riot, which would have been pointless, as the army was nearby. Before his death, Father Stan told the Carmelite Sisters to sing Easter songs with the people if he was killed. And so they did. The Sisters led the people in singing songs about the triumph of Christ's death and resurrection. The prayer and singing channeled the grief away from the blindness of anger.

When it came time to bury him, the people of Santiago Atitlan did not want their beloved pastor's body to return to Oklahoma. They were allowed to keep the heart of their shepherd, which is now enshrined in the church where Father Stan served his people.

LIVE IT

PRUDENCE

PRUDENCE enables one to reason and to act rightly in any given situation —"right reason in action."

A Disciple of Christ living the virtue of prudence...

- ✓ Seeks advice from reasonable and trustworthy persons
- ✓ Carefully considers all circumstances before making a decision
- ✓ Prays about what the Lord would have them do before making a decision
- ✓ Acts upon a sound decision made after thoughtful deliberation

In the words of St. Pope John Paul II...

So a prudent man is not one who—as is often meant—is able to wangle things in life and draw the greatest profit from it; but one who is able to construct his whole life according to the voice of upright conscience and according to the requirements of sound morality.

So prudence is the key for the accomplishment of the fundamental task that each of us has received from God. This task is the perfection of man himself. God has given our humanity to each of us. We must meet this task by planning it accordingly. —St. Pope John Paul II, General Audience, Wednesday, 25 October 1978

Going Deeper in Prudence

FROM THE CATECHISM

Prudence is the virtue that disposes practical reason to discern our true good in every circumstance and to choose the right means of achieving it; "the prudent man looks where he is going" [Proverbs 14:15]. "Keep sane and sober for your prayers" [1 Peter 4:7]. Prudence is "right reason in action," writes St. Thomas Aquinas, following Aristotle [*Summa Theologiae* II–II, 47, 2]. It is not to be confused with timidity or fear, nor with duplicity or dissimulation. It is called *auriga virtutum* (the charioteer of the virtues); it guides the other virtues by setting rule and measure. It is prudence that immediately guides the judgment of conscience. The prudent man determines and directs his conduct in accordance with this judgment. With the help of this virtue we apply moral principles to particular cases without error and overcome doubts about the good to achieve and the evil to avoid (*CCC*, 1806).

Prudence disposes the practical reason to discern, in every circumstance, our true good and to choose the right means for achieving it (*CCC*, 1835).

Quote from St. Thomas Aquinas

St. Thomas of Aquinas' description of a person who lives according to Christian prudence:

One who remains tranquil, "not because she or he is not solicitous about anything, but because the prudent person is not over-anxious about many things, but remains confident and unworried over matters where one ought to have trust" (Romanus Cessario, *The Virtues,* or the *Examined Life* [Continuum, 2002], p. 110, quoting St. Thomas of Aquinas, *Summa Theologiae* IIa–IIae, q. 47, a. 9, ad. 3).

Going Deeper in Prudence

The following sins against prudence impede one from living an ordered lifestyle and growing in emotional maturity:

Worry	Obsessive planning for how to obtain earthly goods and secure one's future needs
Craftiness	Use of false or evil means to gain a desired good
Carnal Prudence	Shrewd pursuit of fleshly goals and one's self-interest

■ **Avarice (greed)** is an inordinate desire of earthly things. This sin causes:

- Treachery
- Fraud
- Deceit
- Perjury
- Restlessness
- Violence
- Hardness of heart, opposed to compassion

■ **Lust** is the inordinate desire for sexual pleasure or inordinate enjoyment of sexual pleasure. This sin causes:

- Blindness of mind
- Inconsideration
- Inconstancy
- Precipitation or hastiness
- Inordinate self-love
- Hatred of God
- Disordered attachment to this present world
- Dread of that which is to come
- Despair

The Blessed Virgin Mary and the Gifts of the Holy Spirit

The Wedding Feast at Cana and the Gift of Counsel

In the Gospel of John, the first miracle of Jesus' ministry is the changing of water into wine at the wedding feast of Cana (see also John 2:1–12). This divine sign inaugurates and signals the impact of God's transforming presence and power in our midst. What happens to that water is meant to happen to us—and even more! Therefore, it is of paramount importance for us to take note of how the Lord changes water into wine.

At the center of the transformation is Mary, the Mother of God. It is Mary who takes notice that the wine has run out. It is Mary who informs her Son of the situation. And, especially, it is Mary who instructs those waiting on table: "Do whatever he tells you" (John 2:5).

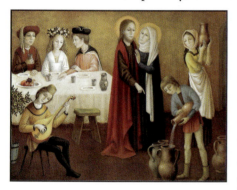

Perhaps the most remarkable aspect of the story is that the waiters actually listen to Mary. They follow her counsel.

The divine Gift of Counsel is the way the Holy Spirit quickens and instructs our minds to do whatever contributes to our spiritual welfare. Counsel is reasoned inquiry that leads us to deliberate action. But in the process, the Holy Spirit safeguards our freedom, our ability to reason things out for ourselves, and our willpower. Notice that the waiters don't heed the Blessed Mother like either tyrannized or obsequious slaves. Rather, they listen intently, intelligently: and they make a choice. We get the sense that there was reflection and sound deliberation at work in the minds and hearts of these servants who were surely impressed by the confidence, the prudence, and the soundness of this remarkable dinner guest—whom they, in turn, decided to obey.

Mary's words of counsel lead the waiters to her Son, and the Gift of Counsel leads us, as well, to Jesus. In our searching for the Lord we need the very guidance of God which the Gift of Counsel supplies. For in this gift we are given God's own advice to make us holy. Everyone who is a friend of God by grace is blessed with God's counsel to advise us what we need to do in matters necessary for our salvation.

There is a risk involved in following the Spirit's counsel. Counsel might instruct us to do things that, in the eyes of the world, seem to make not much sense—like filling water jars and drawing out water for head waiters to taste! Therefore, a profound level of trust is required in order to benefit fully from the Gift of Counsel, the kind of trust that compelled professional waiters to listen to the counsel of a "perfect" stranger and to do whatever her Son told them. We are asked to do no less. And if we do, we can expect to be transformed from waiters into wedding guests who are the first to taste the choice wine that was saved for last.

To benefit from this Gift, we must surrender any stubborn self-reliance that would prevent us from taking God's advice. St. Augustine writes that even the angels consult God about things beneath them. It is a hallmark of the Church to rely on Counsel as a healthy, vital, life-giving dynamic of our life of faith.

The Holy Spirit's Gift of Counsel pertains to everything leading to eternal life. Counsel quickens and instructs our minds to tend to the miraculous Jesus at a wedding feast; at the Feast of his Last Supper where he turns wine into his blood; and to keep on tending him until we are transformed with him at the wedding feast of heaven. The counsel and maternal mediation of Mary keeps us headed in Jesus' direction, especially when she sees something empty or unsatisfied in ourselves that the love of her Son is guaranteed to transform.

"The Wedding Feast at Cana and the Gift of Counsel," pg. 37. Cameron, Peter John O.P. *The Gifts of the Holy Spirit*. Veritas Series. Connecticut: Knights of Columbus, 2002.

ACTING WITH PRUDENCE

RELATED VIRTUE OF PRUDENCE

CIRCUMSPECTION

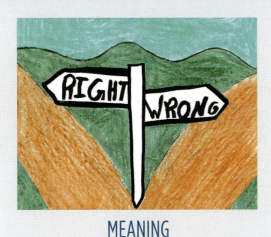

MEANING
Careful consideration of circumstances and consequences

OPPOSING TRAIT
Highlights a pattern of behavior which needs to change in order for one to mature in virtue; considering only oneself when acting

WAYS TO CULTIVATE

AGES 6 AND UP — Pause to think before you say anything. "Let me first think about it."

AGES 10 AND UP — Think before acting and speaking.

AGES 12 AND UP — Seek advice; silently reflect upon the circumstances and consequences of your actions (memory).

SCRIPTURE

Psalm 31:2–6	Matthew 1:18–24
Proverbs 14:8	Luke 14:28–30
Proverbs 22:3	Acts 1:15–26
Sirach 22:27	Acts 5:33–40

SAINTS

Bl. Miguel Pro
DATES: 1891–1927 | **FEAST:** November 23

As a boy Miguel had many friends, and he loved to play practical jokes. He became a priest at a time when the Catholic Church in Mexico was being persecuted. He used his knack for putting together disguises to work undercover and bring the sacraments to many suffering people. He was able to serve his people during this persecution, seeing what was needed at critical moments.

Fr. Miguel Pro died a martyr for the faith.

St. John Baptist de la Salle
DATES: 1651–1719 | **FEAST:** April 7

John lived in France in the seventeenth century. He carefully came up with different methods to help children learn, responding to the needs of both teachers and students to make education a useful and happy process. John saw that it would be better if classes were taught in French instead of Latin. He also encouraged his students to treat each other with respect.

St. Jane Frances de Chantal
DATES: 1572–1641 | **FEAST:** August 18

Jane grew up in a wealthy family and married a loving husband. When he died in a tragic accident, Jane was thrown into a deep grief. St. Francis de Sales helped her to see God's goodness, even in the midst of her sorrows. She slowly began to see God at work in her life and was finally able to forgive the man who caused her husband's accident. Jane later founded a community of sisters. She gave them simple, practical advice, teaching them to do everything for the love of God.

St. Edmund Campion
DATES: 1540–1581 | **FEAST:** December 1

Edmund was smart, successful, and popular when he gave up his career to become a priest. That was a risky thing to do. Queen Elizabeth had passed laws making it illegal to be a priest in England. He went to France to study for the priesthood. Once he was ordained, he snuck back into England disguised as a merchant. He said Masses in secret and administered the sacraments. Pamphlets were popular at the time and many of them attacked the Catholic faith, St. Edmund wrote one and called it *Campion's Brag*. Many people read it because it was encouraging and humorous. It helped the faithful know the truths of their faith and avoid the errors of their time.

PRUDENCE

Prayer

Dear Jesus,

My actions affect not just myself, but others. Please give me the wisdom to think before acting. Please give me the gift of counsel, that I may act in the best way at each moment of the day.

ACTING WITH PRUDENCE

RELATED VIRTUE OF PRUDENCE

DOCILITY

MEANING

Willingness to be taught

OPPOSING TRAIT

Being stubborn, inflexible, and proudly set in one's ways

WAYS TO CULTIVATE

AGES 6 AND UP — Follow directions; be willing to take turns. "Thank you for teaching me."

AGES 10 AND UP — Listen to the teacher; follow directions; be willing to take turns.

AGES 12 AND UP — Listen to others and be willing to follow directions; thank others for rightful corrections.

SCRIPTURE

1 Samuel 3:1–10	Proverbs 15:32	Matthew 7:24–25
2 Samuel 12:13	Sirach 6:32–33	Mark 4:9
Proverbs 12:1	Matthew 5:1–2	Acts 17:11–12

SAINTS

St. Dominic Savio DATES: 1842–1857 | FEAST: May 6

One day young Dominic asked his teacher, St. John Bosco, to teach him how to be a saint. He eagerly listened to everything Don Bosco told him and put it into practice. He wanted Jesus and Mary to be his best friends and would rather die than commit a mortal sin. Several of the boys at the school admired Dominic and thought of him as a friend. He grew quickly in virtue because he was docile and obedient to all that Don Bosco taught him.

St. Juan Diego DATES: 1474–15487 | FEAST: December 9

When the Spanish settlers came to Mexico in the 1500s, missionaries came with them. At first not very many Aztec Indians converted to the faith, but Juan did, and he was very eager to learn about his new faith. He would walk for miles to go to Mass. One day while walking, he heard the voice of a woman calling him. She asked him to tell the bishop to build her a shrine. When Juan went to him, the bishop asked for a sign. Juan Diego returned to the hill and found roses there, even though it was winter. The Lady arranged them in his cloak. When Juan showed the roses to the bishop, a miraculous image of the Lady was on his cloak. A shrine was built there to Our Lady of Guadalupe, and millions of people were converted.

St. Francisco DATES: 1908–1919
St. Jacinta Marto DATES: 1910–19207 | FEAST: February 20

Francisco and Jacinta were brother and sister. Together with their cousin Lucia, they saw Our Lady at Fatima, Portugal, when they were only nine and seven years old. Our Lady and an angel asked them to pray and sacrifice for the salvation of sinners.

The children gave their food to hungry children and offered to Jesus the sacrifice of not playing their favorite games so that sinners could be saved. They obeyed Our Lady in all that she taught them because they loved God.

St. Miguel Febres Cordero DATES: 1854–19107 | FEAST: February 9

Miguel was a teacher who did not mind learning from his students. He was a Christian Brother working in Quito, Ecuador. His students loved him because he always tried to teach them in new ways that they could understand. He was very kind and compassionate to all. Although he was a great scholar and author, his first priority was to teach his students well.

Prayer

Dear Jesus,

You are my teacher in every situation! Before acting on important matters, please give me the humility to seek Your wisdom and the wisdom of others, in order to make the best decision. Give me the gift of counsel, so that I may do Your holy will in each situation.

ACTING WITH PRUDENCE

RELATED VIRTUE OF PRUDENCE

FORESIGHT

MEANING

Consideration of the consequences of one's actions; thinking ahead

OPPOSING TRAIT

Highlights a pattern of behavior which needs to change in order for one to mature in virtue; failing to consider later consequences

WAYS TO CULTIVATE

AGES 6 AND UP	Think about the options: "Let me think about what will happen if…"
AGES 10 AND UP	Learn how to gather information to make a decision; plan ahead for tests and projects.
AGES 12 AND UP	Pray, think, act; learn how to gather information to make a decision; plan out long-term and short-term goals.

SCRIPTURE

Genesis 41:33–36	Matthew 5:25–26	Matthew 26:41
Genesis 23:3–21	Matthew 6:34	Luke 12:54–55
Proverbs 2:1–12	Matthew 7:24–28	Luke 14:28–32
Proverbs 27:12	Matthew 24:32–33	James 3:5–8
Sirach 18:27	Matthew 25:1–13	
Daniel 1:8–14	Matthew 25:14–30	

Prayer

Dear Jesus,
When I come upon situations that require serious thought, please send Your Holy Spirit to guide me, that I may always do Your holy will. Guide me with Your counsel, and give me the courage to act rightly when it is difficult.

SAINTS

St. John Bosco   DATES: 1815–1888 | FEAST: January 31

John devoted himself to training boys how to make a living and teaching them to love God. He believed that, instead of threatening young people with punishments, it was more effective to show them they were loved and trusted. His foresight prevented many young men from falling into evil ways and brought them instead to embrace virtue and holiness.

St. Frances Xavier Cabrini   DATES: 1850–1917 | FEAST: November 13

Maria Francesca wanted to be a sister but was unable to enter the convent. She began working in an orphanage in Italy. The bishop noticed her devotion and holiness and eventually allowed her to make her vows. She noticed that immigrants were in need of help, so she asked the bishop if she could form a group of sisters to serve them. She and her sisters traveled to America to serve the Italian immigrants. In America she founded hospitals, schools, and orphanages to take care of their needs.

Ven. Pope Pius XII   DATES: 1876–1958 | FEAST: Not yet declared

Pope Pius XII was pope during the Second World War, when the Nazi powers were brutally persecuting Christian and Jewish people throughout Europe. Many people tried to tell the Holy Father how to handle the terrible situation, but Pius XII relied primarily on prayer to discern the best way to help those in need. He was heroic in his courage and charity, directing the Church to provide refuge, food, and money to the suffering in various countries. His efforts, although quiet, saved the lives of thousands of people. He even hid Jews at Castel Gandolfo.

St. Gregory the Great   DATES: ca. 540–604 | FEAST: September 3

Gregory, the son of a Roman senator, was governor of Rome when he was called to the religious life. After founding six monasteries, he was elected pope. As the supreme pontiff he worked hard to organize and guide the Church: he created an improved calendar, still in use today, and protected the city from barbarians. He also saved the people from famine by organizing Rome's granaries. He brought more order to sacred music, and the Church continues to appreciate his contributions to the liturgy.

LOVING WITH JUSTICE

JUSTICE

Justice is often represented by a scale because it helps us weigh what is right and fair and to act accordingly. In ancient times, people thought that ideal justice was blind, blind to influence or flattery. Christian justice sees with the eyes of the heart, animated and motivated by charity.

"Blessed are they who hunger and thirst for righteousness, for they will be satisfied."

—Matthew 5:6

RELATED VIRTUES:

AFFABILITY   COURTESY   GENEROSITY   GRATITUDE   KINDNESS

LOYALTY   OBEDIENCE   PATRIOTISM   PRAYERFULNESS   RESPECT

RESPONSIBILITY   SINCERITY   TRUSTWORTHINESS

JUSTICE

KNOW IT

LOVING WITH JUSTICE

> **JUSTICE** enables one to give to each, beginning with God, what is due him.

Justice is the cardinal virtue that perfects our will and all our relationships with others, including family, country, and Church. It is the constant and firm will to give to each what is his due. It disposes us to respect the rights and dignity of others, leading to harmony and equality in human interactions. Justice toward God is the virtue of religion. The just Christian is motivated by charity, a sincere will to not only give to others what is their due, but to will the good for them.

Cardinal Virtue of Justice

CCC, 2408
CCC, 2409
CCC, 2412
CCC, 1807
CCC, 1836

Summa Theologiae

II–II.Q57–122, St. Thomas Aquinas

Echoing the Mystery

49–Cardinal Virtue of Justice

> **Particular Justice** gives particular (or specific) goods to an individual or group.

Distributive Justice	Commutative Justice
Distributive justice is concerned about the distribution of common goods. Common goods, such as safety, peace, access to food and housing, are those things that are necessary for all members of a society or community.	Commutative justice is concerned about the proper handling of an individual's private goods. Private goods, such as private property, a person's income, someone's good name, are privately owned and regulated by individuals.
The leaders of societies and communities are responsible for the fair and proportional distribution of common goods to their members. This may be the parents of a family, the boss of a factory, or the government of a country.	Private individuals are responsible for the fair exchange of goods among each other. If they violate this—such as by theft, vandalism, or gossip—they are responsible to make up for the damage (restitution) as well as the injury done to the other (satisfaction).
Example: *A small, poor nation just suffered a massive earthquake. People around the world send food, clothing, and medical supplies to the nation's capital to give to the people in need. If the government is just, it will fairly distribute the supplies to those in need.*	*Example:* *There are two girls in seventh grade. One spreads rumors about the other on social media. The next day, the girl's friends abandon her because they were horrified by the rumors. To make restitution, the first girl needs to tell others that the rumors were not true. She should find some way to apologize and work to rebuild the girl's good reputation.*

Key Points
- Aims to perfect our wills and relationships
- Respects the rights and dignity of others
- Justice toward God is the virtue of religion

JUSTICE

GUARD IT

The cardinal virtue of justice aims to perfect all our relationships. At our Baptism, our heavenly Father gave us this virtue to aid us in maintaining a balance. The sins against justice cause an imbalance or inequality in relationships. Like any virtue, justice must be guarded from sins. The following are some sins that need to be guarded against:

Sins Against Distributive Justice	Sins Against Commutative Justice
• Lack of respect for others • Favoritism, such being unfair in law enforcement • Accepting bribery, allowing corruption • Discrimination • Perjury	• Lack of respect for others • Causing bodily harm, such as self-harm, mutilation, bullying, abortion, murder • Causing damage to property, such as vandalism or theft • Causing damage to one's reputation, such as defamation, detraction, gossip, ridicule, cursing, bullying (including cyber bullying)

A Note About Speech

Each person has a right to a good reputation. A common way that we sin against justice is in speech.

- **Defamation** is openly taking away from one someone's character—i.e., a false statement posted publicly.
- **Detraction** is privately taking from someone's reputation.
- **Gossip** is conversing maliciously about a person.
- **Ridicule** is heaping insult publicly on another.
- **Cursing** is uttering evil against someone, either ordering it or wishing it.

St. Thomas Aquinas states there are four ways by which one can detract from another's reputation:

1. Attributing what is false to him
2. Exaggerating his sins
3. Exposing secrets
4. Saying that good actions have been motivated by evil intentions

   (Romanus Cessario, *The Virtues or Examined Life* [Continuum, 2002], p.141, quoting St. Thomas Aquinas, *Summa theologiae* IIa–IIae, q. 73, a. 1, ad 3)

> *Christ instructs us in divine justice and goodness, telling us to be like our heavenly Father, holy, perfect and merciful. "Forgive," he says, "and you will be forgiven. Behave toward other people as you would wish them to behave toward you."*
> —St. Maximus the Confessor

> "The tongue is hard to tame."
> —James 3:7–8

Tips For Taming The Tongue:

T Is this true?
H Is this helpful?
I Is this inspiring?
N Is this necessary?
K Is this kind?

JUSTICE

KNOW IT

GIFT OF PIETY

RELATED BEATITUDE

The Gift of Piety

"Blessed are the meek, for they shall inherit the earth." —Matthew 5:5

"Blessed are the merciful, for they shall obtain mercy." —Matthew 5:7

Piety fills man with a desire to perform works of mercy because the best way to honor God is to serve the children of God.

Summa Theologiae

II–II.Q101, 121, St. Thomas Aquinas

Piety inclines one as a child of God to have devotion and honor to God as Father.

The cardinal virtue of justice enables one to give to each what is owed to him. The **Gift of Piety** gives a tenderness and a devotion to the worship we owe God. Worship, inspired by Piety, is not just required because He is our Lord, but something that we desire because He is our Father who loves us. Piety gives a disciple new eyes with which to see his neighbor. Each person is my brother or sister, a beloved child of our heavenly Father. Piety inspires trust in the Father and gives peace and joy to the children of God.

Effects of the Gift of the Holy Spirit

- Wants to go beyond duty
- Gives a promptness to do the will of the Father
- Inspires reverence and devotion in worship and prayer

GUARD IT

The cardinal virtue of justice and the Gift of Piety are gifts given us at Baptism. Understanding the manifestations of the capital sin of pride will assist is guarding justice and piety.

Pride: An excessive self-love closes off our hearts, causing a person to make himself the center of his own reality. This leads to a **hardness of heart,** where the person is unable to delight in the goodness of God and others. He cannot feel compassion for others or put up with their faults, and thus becomes impatient with them. He loses a sense of affection for God and no longer feels sorrow for his sins.

PRAY IT *LECTIO DIVINA*

Matthew 20:1–16

"The kingdom of heaven is like a landowner who went out at dawn to hire laborers for his vineyard. After agreeing with them for the usual daily wage, he sent them into his vineyard. Going out about nine o'clock, he saw others standing idle in the marketplace, and he said to them, 'You too go into my vineyard, and I will give you what is just.' So they went off. [And] he went out again around noon, and around three o'clock, and did likewise. Going out about five o'clock, he found others standing around, and said to them, 'Why do you stand here idle all day?' They answered, 'Because no one has hired us.' He said to them, 'You too go into my vineyard.' When it was evening the owner of the vineyard said to his foreman, 'Summon the laborers and give them their pay, beginning with the last and ending with the first.' When those who had started about five o'clock came, each received the usual daily wage. So when the first came, they thought that they would receive more, but each of them also got the usual wage. And on receiving it they grumbled against the landowner, saying, 'These last ones worked only one hour, and you have made them equal to us, who bore the day's burden and the heat.' He said to one of them in reply, 'My friend, I am not cheating you. Did you not agree with me for the usual daily wage? Take what is yours and go. What if I wish to give this last one the same as you? [Or] am I not free to do as I wish with my own money? Are you envious because I am generous?' Thus, the last will be first, and the first will be last."

1. God's Word strikes the heart. What word or phrase touched your heart?
2. Justice is giving God and neighbor their due. How did the landowner practice justice toward his hired laborers?
3. From a human perspective it is understandable that the laborers grumbled against the landowner. Do you think the landowner was just or does he act justly with mercy?
4. Re-read the passage taking to heart Jesus' message describing the kingdom of Heaven. How is God's justice and mercy revealed?
5. Ask this question in prayer: "Jesus, it can be difficult to understand how the landowner acted with justice. How does my heart need to change so that I may not complain when others may receive the same or more?" Write down what He says to you.

Pray an Act of Justice

Dear God,

You are the Author of all life, and I give You praise.
Help me see and serve You in everyone I meet today.

JUSTICE

LIVE IT LOOKING TO THE SAINTS

ST. KATHARINE DREXEL

Christian justice is rooted in the fact that each person is created in the image and likeness of God and destined for eternal happiness. And so, each person has inestimable dignity. When this reality shapes how we interact with people, Christian justice can defy the expectations of human society.

Katharine Drexel was born in 1858, the daughter of a wealthy Philadelphia banker and philanthropist. Her parents had a uniquely Christian understanding of wealth and its attending responsibilities. They intentionally formed their three daughters in generosity, service, and humility. They brought the poor and destitute into their home. There, they were honored guests and the family served for themselves. It is estimated that her mother spent $11 million in the service of the poor. Katharine and her sisters grew up knowing how to see the dignity of the person in the poor.

> **Loving with Justice**
>
> Katharine and her sisters grew up knowing how to see the dignity of the person in the poor.

Katharine's father died in 1885 and the young ladies found themselves the heirs of a vast fortune, close to $400 million in today's terms. She and her sisters went on a tour of the American West, where Katherine was financing several schools. Katharine was deeply moved by the poverty and suffering of the Native Americans. The public sentiment of the 1880s ran against the Native Americans as the United States Army waged various campaigns against them. The plight of the African Americans in post-Civil War South also pulled at her sense of justice.

In 1893 Katharine and her sisters went on a European tour. They obtained an audience with Pope Leo XIII where the young heiress asked that missionaries be sent to the Native Americans. The pope turned the tables on her by asking her to become the missionary.

Katharine soon did, shocking Philadelphia society by joining a convent. With the help of Bishop James O'Connor, she drafted a constitution for a community of sisters who would serve the African and Native Americans. She recognized that all social justice is inherently Eucharistic, that the eyes of faith that see Christ in the form of bread should also be able to see Him in the marginalized of society. In 1891 she made her vows as the first Sister of the Blessed Sacrament.

Over the next sixty years Katharine and her sisters opened one hundred and forty-five missions, forty-nine elementary schools, and twelve high school. By 1937, she was confined to a wheelchair. The heiress of Philadelphia practiced radical personal poverty. She made her wheelchair from a simple kitchen chair and wheels from an abandoned baby carriage. The last twenty years of her life were spent in prayer and adoration. She died in 1955 at the age of ninety-six.

LIVE IT

JUSTICE

JUSTICE enables one to give to each, beginning with God, what is due him.

A Disciple of Christ living the virtue of justice...

- ✓ Shows devotion and honor to God as Father
- ✓ Offers to God what one has done
- ✓ Lifts one's heart and mind to God through prayer (praise, contrition, thanksgiving, and supplication)
- ✓ Respects oneself
- ✓ Treats others with respect, recognizing the innate dignity of each person
- ✓ Distributes to each what is necessary in a manner that is honorable
- ✓ Is obedient, loyal, and respectful to those in authority
- ✓ Pays due honor with respect to one's country with a willingness to serve

In the words of St. Pope John Paul II...

It is necessary, therefore, to deepen our knowledge of justice continually. It is not a theoretical science. It is virtue, it is capacity of the human spirit, of the human will and also of the heart. It is also necessary to pray in order to be just and to know how to be just.

We cannot forget Our Lord's words: "The measure you give will be the measure you get" (Matthew 7:2).

A just man is a man of a "just measure." —St. Pope John Paul II, General Audience, Wednesday, 8 November 1978

Going Deeper in Justice

FROM THE CATECHISM

Justice is the moral virtue that consists in the constant and firm will to give their due to God and neighbor. Justice toward God is called the "virtue of religion." Justice toward men disposes one to respect the rights of each and to establish in human relationships the harmony that promotes equity with regard to persons and to the common good. The just man, often mentioned in the Sacred Scriptures, is distinguished by habitual right thinking and the uprightness of his conduct toward his neighbor. "You shall not be partial to the poor or defer to the great, but in righteousness shall you judge your neighbor" [Leviticus 19:25]. "Masters, treat your slaves justly and fairly, knowing that you also have a Master in heaven" [Colossians 4:1] (*CCC*, 1807).

Virtues Allied to Justice

Virtues of Veneration: These virtues regulate the conduct toward those in positions of authority.

Religion	Filial Piety	Respect
The theological virtue of charity gives life to the cardinal virtues. Charity prompts us to adore God. The virtue of religion enables us to give due worship to God.	Children owe their parents a certain respect and obedience. Piety "softens" it, giving tenderness to the relationship.	The virtue of respect enables us to speak and act according to our own and others' rights, status, and circumstances.

Going Deeper in Justice

- **Virtue of Civility:** Civility regulates interpersonal relationships among those in society. Truth and gratitude regulate human interaction. Affability and liberality (an ability to acquit debts that strict justice does not require) are personal characteristics that contribute to a happier experience of daily life.

Virtue of Religion (*CCC*, 2095–2103)

Virtue of Religion: This virtue, when animated by charity, manifests itself in these actions:

Adoration	The supreme homage and worship given to God alone
Prayer	The lifting of one's heart and mind to God spending time with Him; prayers of adoration, contrition, thanksgiving, and supplication (petition)
Sacrifice	Making an offering in loving conversation to God
Promises	A simple resolution or commitment made to God regarding one's actions or prayer
Vows	A deliberate and free promise made to God that is binding (Religious take vows of the evangelical counsels of poverty, chastity, and obedience.)

The Blessed Virgin Mary and the Gifts of the Holy Spirit

The Visitation of Mary and the Gift of Piety

Immediately after Gabriel left her presence, "Mary set out, proceeding in haste into the hill country to a town of Judah, where she entered Zechariah's house, and greeted her kinswoman Elizabeth" (Luke 1:39–40). In so doing, Mary manifests the Spirit's Gift of Piety that prepares God's people to be promptly responsive in a special way to the divine inspirations he sends. Mary's love of her cherished relationship with God moves her immediately to offer him extraordinary homage and worship. And it should move us as well.

The visitation is an act that manifests the Gift of Piety. Piety concerns fulfilling our duty and conscientious service toward God, toward our country, and toward those related to us by blood or by any common allegiance. The visitation gives expression to the Blessed Mother's love for God, for the child in her womb, for her relatives Elizabeth and Zechariah, for the child in Elizabeth's womb, and for the common allegiance they all share thanks to the divine vocations with which they have been entrusted.

Above all else, the Gift of Piety is the offering of special service and honor to God as Father. Elizabeth proclaims the unique honor and service Mary offers to God: "Blessed are you who trusted that the Lord's words to her would be fulfilled" (Luke 1:45). And Mary's Magnificat (cf. Luke 1:46–55) praises the greatness of God's fatherly care, especially as he brings to fulfillment all that "he promised our fathers, promised Abraham and his descendants forever" (Luke 1:55). Mary's piety proclaims

how God as a Father fulfills his promises to the Old Testament fathers. Whenever we join in proclaiming Mary's Magnificat, we more deeply esteem our own relationship with God in the most profound words of worship and honor.

Piety is also concerned with coming to the aid of those in need. St. Augustine wrote that we pay homage to those whom we cherish by doing honor either to their memory or their company. Mary exercises the chief act of piety by bringing her Son to Elizabeth—and to us—out of reverence for God. But at the same time, the Blessed Mother's offering to Elizabeth is also an offering to God. Elizabeth is vividly aware of this: "Who am I that the mother of my Lord should come to me?" This pious exclamation of Elizabeth reveals another dimension of the gift: Piety moves us to honor the indebtedness we bear to others because of their superiority in our life as well as because of the different benefits they contribute to our life. Elizabeth's piety toward Mary—and therefore to God the Father—expresses her indebtedness to Mary by honoring the Blessed Mother as our God-given source of new life, holiness, and joy. We are called to take up Elizabeth's pious regard for Mary as a way of cultivating the Gift of Piety in our own souls. Just as Mary and Elizabeth show honor to each other, so too do the saints demonstrate this kind of piety in heaven to each other as well as to us on earth by the compassion they show to us in our moments of misery.

Through the Gift of Piety, the Holy Spirit inspires us to have a profoundly childlike attitude toward God. Mary and Elizabeth, at this moment, are childlike in a unique way, for they are actually with child. The gift of piety calls us to be childlike as well. And as we respond to that gift by honoring God as Father, we can be assured in our littleness with Mary that "God will raise the lowly to high places" (Luke 1:52).

"The Visitation of Mary and the Gift of Piety," pg. 32. Cameron, Peter John O.P. *The Gifts of the Holy Spirit*. Veritas Series. Connecticut: Knights of Columbus, 2002.

LOVING WITH JUSTICE

RELATED VIRTUE OF JUSTICE

AFFABILITY

MEANING
Being easy to approach and easy to talk to—friendly

OPPOSING TRAIT
Being mean, unkind, cruel, or unflattering

WAYS TO CULTIVATE

AGES 6 AND UP — Smile; greet people. "How are you doing?"

AGES 10 AND UP — Smile; acknowledge the presence of others; take time to listen to others.

AGES 12 AND UP — Smile; acknowledge the presence of others, both peers and adults; try to see Jesus in others.

Scripture

2 Kings 2:2
Job 2:11
Proverbs 17:17
Ecclesiastes 4:9–10
Matthew 7:12
Matthew 18:1–4
Matthew 19:13–14
Mark 10:16
Mark 10:21
Luke 1:39–42, 44
Luke 19:5–7
Luke 24:13–35
John 1:35–39
John 4:7–15, 27–30, 39–42
Colossians 3:12–14
1 Thessalonians 5:11

SAINTS

Bl. Pier Giorgio Frassati DATES: 1901–1925 | FEAST: July 4

As a young man in Italy, Pier Giorgio loved mountain climbing and hiking in the outdoors. He was cheerful and friendly, ready to listen to all he met. He never complained about his personal struggles or told people how much he helped the poor. When he was only twenty-four, he died of polio. No one realized how many friends he had, especially among the poor, until large crowds came to his funeral.

St. Francis of Assisi DATES: 1181–1226 | FEAST: October 4

Francis was a fun-loving, wealthy young man when the Lord intervened and gave him a new love, Lady Poverty. Francis initially wanted to live as a hermit, loving God in solitude. However, his cheerfulness and joy attracted people. They marveled that a man so poor could be so friendly. Many people asked if they could join him. He called his followers the "Little Brothers," or "Friars Minor." Today they are known as the Franciscans.

Bl. Jordan of Saxony DATES: 1190–1237 | FEAST: February 13

Jordan was a Dominican friar who, upon St. Dominic's death, became the head of the order. Jordan often went out to preach, and he would come back with many young men who were ready to enter the Dominican life. Jordan's friendly, approachable manner inspired many to give their lives to God, and thus he added great numbers to this new Order of Preachers.

St. Gabriel of the Sorrowful Mother (Francis Possenti)
DATES: 1838–1862 | FEAST: July 4

Francis was known to his friends as a cheerful, popular boy who enjoyed the latest books and plays. He entered the Passionist Order and took the name Gabriel of the Sorrowful Mother. His love and devotion to the Crucified Christ and His Sorrowful Mother didn't turn him into a somber or serious man. Instead, those who know him believed him to be a saint, not because he did anything great, but because in normal daily life he was always joyful.

Prayer

Jesus, King of my heart,
You were kind to the little children who came to You. Be my strength as I try to be good to all those I meet today.

LOVING WITH JUSTICE

RELATED VIRTUE OF JUSTICE
COURTESY

MEANING

Treating other people with respect, recognizing that all are made in God's image and likeness

OPPOSING TRAIT

Not recognizing the inherent dignity of others made in God's image and likeness

WAYS TO CULTIVATE

AGES 6 AND UP
Let others go first.
"You can go first." "Let's work together."

AGES 10 AND UP
Practice manners; let others go first; speak in a gentle, patient tone; do not interrupt.

AGES 12 AND UP
Show awareness of the feelings of others; be polite; go out of your way for others.

Scripture

Genesis 18:1–5	Acts 15:12–14	1 Timothy 5:1–2
Proverbs 20:3	Ephesians 4:29	Titus 3:1–2
Sirach 31:16–19	Ephesians 4:32	Hebrews 13:2
Luke 1:39–42	Colossians 4:6	Revelation 3:20
Luke 14:7–11		

SAINTS

St. Paulinus of Nola DATES: 354–431 | FEAST: June 22

Paulinus was a successful politician in Gaul at the end of the Roman Empire. When he became a Christian, he gave all his time and wealth to the Church. Everyone loved him for his kindness and courtesy. His fellow Christians asked him to become a priest. He served them faithfully as a priest and was made a bishop.

St. Nicholas DATES: ca. 270–346 | FEAST: December 6

Nicholas became the bishop of Myra, Turkey. He was known for his generosity and compassion to the poor. He often performed his works of mercy secretly, so no one would be embarrassed by receiving help. One time there was a poor man who could not afford for his daughters to make good marriages. Nicholas secretly put three bags of money in their house, keeping the daughters from a life of servitude.

St. Rose of Lima DATES: 1586–1617 | FEAST: August 23

Rose was still very young when Jesus asked her to consecrate herself to Him. Her family didn't understand why she began acting differently. She spent long hours in prayer and practiced many sacrifices. People from all over the city would come to talk to her and ask her to pray for them. She took care of the garden, growing vegetables, herbs, and flowers for her family and the poor.

St. Vincent de Paul DATES: 1581–1660 | FEAST: September 27

Vincent had a very eventful life. He grew up on a farm in France. After he became a priest, he was asked to serve as a chaplain to the queen. One day while traveling by sea, his ship was attacked by pirates and Vincent was captured as a slave. He eventually escaped and returned to France. These diverse experiences taught Vincent to see the dignity of each person, rich or poor. The example of his own courtesy has inspired people to serve the poor, especially by giving them clothing and food.

Prayer

Dear Jesus,
Help me to show respect toward others in my words, manners, and body language.

LOVING WITH JUSTICE
RELATED VIRTUE OF JUSTICE
GENEROSITY

SAINTS

St. Fabiola
DATES: Died 399 | **FEAST:** December 27

Fabiola was a rich noblewoman in ancient Rome and a friend of St. Jerome. She gave the Church all her wealth, and her time and efforts as well. She founded a hospital in Rome, where she cared for the poor and the sick. This was very unusual for a rich woman in those times.

St. Martin of Tours
DATES: 316–397 | **FEAST:** November 11

One cold winter day, as Martin was riding through a city on his magnificent horse, he saw a beggar on the side of the road. The beggar had on only light clothes, so Martin took off his warm, thick military cloak and cut it in half, giving half to the beggar. That night he saw a vision of Christ wearing the half cloak. Christ thanked Martin for his great generosity to the poor, because in giving to them, Martin was giving to Christ also.

Martin was once robbed while traveling through a mountainous area. He managed to convert one of the thieves.

Martin became a hermit, but he was so loved and respected that the people of Tours made him their bishop.

St. Elizabeth of Hungary
DATES: 1207–1231 | **FEAST:** November 17

When Elizabeth was young, she married the prince of Thuringia. He loved her for her kind manner and devotion to God, but his family didn't approve. She spent hours in prayer in the castle chapel and took clothing and food to give to the poor. One day her husband's relatives and friends complained to the prince that Elizabeth was giving away too much food. When he went to her, the bread in her basket had turned to roses. From that day on, her husband supported her acts of generosity.

St. Giuseppe Moscati
DATES: 1880–1927 | **FEAST:** November 16

Giuseppe Moscati was an Italian doctor in the early 1900s. He worked hard to get to know his patients personally and bring them back to the sacraments as well as to physical health. Often he would not accept payment from his poor patients, or he would secretly slip their money back to them with their medicine so as not to embarrass them. Dr. Moscati also trained younger doctors to be generous in caring for both the emotional and spiritual needs of their patients.

MEANING
Giving of oneself in a willing and cheerful manner for the good of others

OPPOSING TRAIT
Giving without a spirit of cheer, in a begrudging manner

WAYS TO CULTIVATE

AGES 6 AND UP: Share your items and time. "Would you like to have one of my cookies?"

AGES 10 AND UP: Share; give away extra items.

AGES 12 AND UP: Give of yourself; focus on one act of charity/kindness each day.

Scripture

Leviticus 25:35–37	Matthew 25:34–40	Luke 6:38
Tobit 4:7–8	Luke 1:38	Luke 21:1–4
Psalm 41:1–3	Luke 6:30–31	2 Corinthians 9:6–8
Proverbs 19:17	Luke 6:36	Philippians 2:4
Matthew 10:42		

Prayer

Dear Jesus,
Let me share myself with others as You share Your life with me.

LOVING WITH JUSTICE

RELATED VIRTUE OF JUSTICE

GRATITUDE

MEANING

Thankful disposition of mind and heart

OPPOSING TRAIT

Not expressing appreciation; taking other people and things for granted

WAYS TO CULTIVATE

AGES 6 AND UP — Smile at your mom after she cooks dinner. "Thank you!" "I am thankful for…"

AGES 10 AND UP — Write a thank you note; take into consideration the blessings in your life.

AGES 12 AND UP — Say thank you even for difficult or unwanted things (homework, cleaning your room, etc.); count the blessings in your life.

Scripture

Tobit 13	Luke 1:46–55	Colossians 2:6–7
Psalm 9:1	Luke 17:11–19	1 Thessalonians 5:18
Psalm 50:23	Luke 22:14–20	James 1:2–4
Psalm 118:28–29		

SAINTS

Bl. Solanus Casey
DATES: 1870–1957 | **FEAST:** Not yet declared

Solanus was a Capuchin friar in the United States who spent most of his life as a porter (or doorkeeper) at the midwestern friaries in which he lived. Although many people considered him unintelligent, he never allowed this to make him angry. Instead he was always grateful to God for His many blessings. Fr. Solanus frequently said, "Thank God ahead of time," because he knew that God would always do good to those who love Him.

St. Josephine Bakhita
DATES: ca. 1869–1947 | **FEAST:** February 8

When Josephine was a little girl, she was captured by slave traders in Sudan. The experience was so traumatic that she even forgot her name. The slave traders named her Bakhita, which means "lucky." Over the next several years, she suffered under many cruel masters. Eventually she was purchased by an Italian family, and for the first time she could remember, she was treated kindly. She saw a crucifix and was moved by the fact that "God loved us so much he would suffer for us." She was baptized and later became a sister. Her life was marked by gratitude to God. She said she was even grateful for her sufferings as a slave because she was able to offer them to Jesus.

St. Mary Magdalene
DATES: First Century | **FEAST:** July 22

The Gospel of Luke tells us that Jesus cast seven demons out of Mary Magdalene (see Luke 8:2). Her gratitude for Christ's loving deliverance led her to become His faithful follower. She stood faithfully at the foot of Jesus' cross with Mary and John. She came early to His tomb the next morning to anoint His body, and thus she became the first of His followers to learn that Christ had risen!

St. Augustine
DATES: 354–430 | **FEAST:** August 28

Augustine was born to a pagan father and a Christian mother. Sadly, he followed more in his father's ways than his mother's and became a real troublemaker, even teaching pagan beliefs to others. Eventually his mother's prayers won his conversion. In his immense gratitude for knowing the truth, loving God and loving his Catholic faith, he gave his whole life to God as a priest and later a bishop. St. Augustine wrote so well about God that he was named a Doctor of the Church.

Prayer

Dear Jesus,

Please give me a thankful heart, realizing that all I have comes from You.

LOVING WITH JUSTICE

RELATED VIRTUE OF JUSTICE

KINDNESS

MEANING

Expressing genuine concern for the well-being of others and anticipating their needs

OPPOSING TRAIT

Not regarding the well-being of others, being cruel in looks, words, and actions

WAYS TO CULTIVATE

AGES 6 AND UP — Talk to someone who seems sad. "Do you need any help?"

AGES 10 AND UP — Ask how someone is doing; respond to kindness by being kind in return.

AGES 12 AND UP — Practice speaking, thinking, and acting kindly even when someone is not being kind to you.

Scripture

Genesis 24:14
Exodus 2:16–17
Deuteronomy 7:8–9
2 Samuel 2:4–6
Matthew 10:42
Mark 14:3–6
Luke 4:38–39
Luke 10:33–35
John 2:3–11

SAINTS

St. Aelred of Rievaulx — DATES: ca. 1109–ca. 1166 | FEAST: February 12

When he was growing up, Aelred spent several years in the court of the king of England. He left the fame of the court to become a Cistercian monk. In the monastery his sympathy and kindness toward others were quickly noticed.

Aelred became master of novices and helped educate the young monks. After this he became the abbot of all three hundred monks in the community. He is remembered for his gentleness and patience with each monk under his care

St. Veronica — DATES: First Century | FEAST: July 12

Tradition gives us a woman named Veronica who wiped the face of Jesus with her veil as He bore His cross to Calvary. The soldiers were treating Our Lord cruelly, and everyone feared getting in their way. Veronica, however, saw the Lord's pain and thought that wiping the blood and sweat from his face might aid him a little. The image of the Lord's face was left on her veil. Her kind act is remembered in the sixth Station of the Cross.

St. Martin de Porres — DATES: 1579–1639 | FEAST: November 3

Martin grew up very poor in Peru in the sixteenth century. He became a brother in the Dominican monastery. He took care of animals as well as the cooking and manual labor. Everyone in the city loved him because of his kindness, especially to the poor. He saved novices from getting in trouble and took care of the sick and the poor.

St. Camillus de Lellis — DATES: 1550–1614 | FEAST: July 18

Camillus had a hard childhood, and by his teenage years he was argumentative and proud. He had to go to a local hospital for his diseased leg, but he was so unkind they asked him to leave. He spent the next several years getting in and out of trouble. Then he heard a priest preach about conversion, and Camillus felt God's grace inspiring him to change his life.

Camillus still went to hospitals because of his diseased leg, but he was a different patient now. He began taking care of others or spending time with them so they would not be afraid or lonely. He founded a religious order of brothers to take care of the sick. At the end of his life, he left his own hospital bed to see if other patients needed anything.

Prayer

Dear Jesus,

You are kindness itself. I desire to show charity toward my neighbor through my thoughts, words, and actions. When others meet me, let them meet YOU in me!

LOVING WITH JUSTICE

RELATED VIRTUE OF JUSTICE

LOYALTY

MEANING

Accepting the bonds implicit in relationships; defending virtues upheld by Church, family, and country

OPPOSING TRAIT

Breaking bonds of trust with Church, family, country, friends, and school

WAYS TO CULTIVATE

AGES 6 AND UP — Speak positively about family and friends. "My brother/sister/friend is good at…"

AGES 10 AND UP — Make your actions correspond to your words and promises.

AGES 12 AND UP — Seek to do your best to help others; fulfill your responsibilities; be faithful to your commitments.

Scripture

Ruth 1:15–17
2 Samuel 9:1–7
1 Kings 8:61
2 Kings 2:2
Proverbs 3:1–3
Proverbs 18:24
Proverbs 17:17
Isaiah 6:1–14
2 Maccabees 7:1–2
John 6:66–69
1 Corinthians 13:7
Ephesians 6:14
1 Timothy 3:14–15

SAINTS

St. John Fisher — DATES: d. 1469–1535 | FEAST: June 22

In the sixteenth century Henry VIII, the king of England, rejected the Catholic Church and the pope and began his own church. The king tried to force all the Catholic bishops to join the Church of England, but John remained faithful to the Catholic Church. This led to his execution.

St. Polycarp — DATES: ca. 69–ca. 155 | FEAST: February 23

Polycarp became a disciple of the apostle John when John was very old. Polycarp learned the faith well and then began to teach others. He was arrested by the Romans, who told him to swear an oath by the pagan gods and they would set him free. Polycarp's brave response was, "I have served my King for eighty-six years, and He has never done me wrong. Why should I betray Him now?" His loyalty to Christ cost him his life but brought him glory in heaven.

St. Basil — DATES: 329–379
St. Gregory Nazianzen — DATES: 329–390 | FEAST: January 2

Basil and Gregory met when they were at school together in Athens, and they became close friends. Basil began a monastery and Gregory joined him as a monk. Later Basil was made a bishop and had to leave the monastery. Nearby was a diocese that was not very faithful to the Church. It needed a bishop who would be loyal to Church teaching. Basil asked Gregory to be the bishop there. At first Gregory objected but, out of loyalty to his friend and the Church, he eventually accepted.

St. Ignatius of Loyola — DATES: 1491–1556 | FEAST: July 31

Ignatius was a Spanish soldier, eager for fame, pleasure, and worldly glory. In a battle with the French, his knee was severely injured. During his long recovery he read several books, mostly about heroic knights and their adventures. Then he started reading books about the saints. He realized that being holy was a far more exciting adventure than being a soldier. After his recovery, he gave his whole life to Jesus. He founded the Society of Jesus. Many of his priests became great missionaries who always wanted to give glory to Jesus like St. Ignatius taught them.

Prayer

Dear Jesus,

Help me to be steadfast in my relationships and faithful to the duties those relationships entail, even when this may be difficult.

LOVING WITH JUSTICE

RELATED VIRTUE OF JUSTICE

OBEDIENCE

MEANING

Assenting to rightful authority without hesitation or resistance

OPPOSING TRAIT

Resisting the directives of rightful authority

WAYS TO CULTIVATE

AGES 6 AND UP	Listen; follow directions. "I would be happy to do that for you!"
AGES 10 AND UP	Listen; follow directions the first time they are given and without complaint.
AGES 12 AND UP	Listen to rightful authority; follow directions the first time without complaining and in a prompt manner; anticipate what is expected of you.

Scripture

Exodus 20:1–17	Sirach 3:1–6	Philippians 2:5–8
Exodus 40:16–33	Matthew 24:45–51	Colossians 3:20
Deuteronomy 11:1	Luke 1:38	Titus 3:1
1 Samuel 15:17–22	Luke 2:51–52	Hebrews 11:1–11
Psalm 40:7–9	Romans 5:19	1 Peter 2:13–14
Psalm 119:33–35	Ephesian 6:1–3	James 1:25

SAINTS

St. Claude de la Colombière   DATES: 1641–1682 | FEAST: February 15

Claude was a French Jesuit in the middle of the seventeenth century. As a Jesuit, he pledged complete obedience to his superior, who he viewed as an ambassador of Christ. This obedience gave him the freedom to be confident that he was doing God's will for his life, whether he was being imprisoned for a crime he did not commit or spreading devotion to the Sacred Heart.

St. Padre Pio   DATES: 1887–1968 | FEAST: September 23

Pio of Pietrelcina was an Italian Capuchin priest known affectionately as "Padre Pio." God gave him several extraordinary graces and favors. He received the stigmata (the wounds of Christ), could read souls, bi-locate, and work many miracles. Not everyone believed that Padre Pio's abilities came from God. There were several rumors and false accusations. For a time, his superiors forbade him from doing the two most important tasks of a priest: saying public Mass and hearing confessions. He obeyed without complaint and did all that was asked of him. Soon his superiors recognized the falseness of the accusations and restored his faculties as a priest.

St. Catherine Labouré   DATES: 1806–1876 | FEAST: November 28

As a young sister in her convent in Paris, Catherine had a vision of the Blessed Mother. Mary showed her the Miraculous Medal and told her to have it made. Catherine had to convince a lot of people in order to carry out the Blessed Mother's request. Eventually her superiors, confessor, and the archbishop approved and the medal was made. Afterwards Catherine went back to her hidden quiet life. She took care of the convent chickens, answered the door, and was ready to do whatever was asked of her.

St. Matthew   DATES: First Century | FEAST: September 21

Matthew, also known as Levi, was a tax collector in Judea at the time of Jesus. One day as he sat at his work, Jesus saw him and said to him, "Follow me." Matthew immediately left his work and his friends to obey the Lord's command. He became one of the apostles, an evangelist, and a martyr for Jesus.

Prayer

Dear Jesus,

You are God, and yet You were obedient to Mary and Joseph. Help me to do all that my parents and teachers ask of me—promptly, joyfully, and completely. This virtue pleases You more than all other sacrifices!

LOVING WITH JUSTICE

RELATED VIRTUE OF JUSTICE

PATRIOTISM

MEANING

Paying due honor and respect to one's country with a willingness to serve

OPPOSING TRAIT

Lacking regard or respect for one's country and national symbols

WAYS TO CULTIVATE

AGES 6 AND UP — Show respect for your country's flag. "I pledge allegiance to the flag…"

AGES 10 AND UP — Show respect for people and symbols representing your country; pray for leaders and soldiers.

AGES 12 AND UP — Show respect for symbols and things associated with your country; pray for your country and servicemen.

Scripture

Exodus 12:25–27   Ezra 3:10–11   John 11:55–56
1 Samuel 1:1,3   Psalm 128:5–6   1 Peter 2:13–17

SAINTS

St. Louis IX   DATES: 14214–1270 | FEAST: August 25

Louis IX was a great French king who combined his love of Christ and the Church with a willingness to serve his country. He protected and helped the French priests, set up shelters and hospitals for the poor and sick, and built beautiful churches for the people of France. He also gave thought to his own prayer life, spending many hours in prayer for himself and his country.

St. Thomas à Becket   DATES: 1118–1170 | FEAST: December 29

Thomas was a good friend of Henry II, King of England. Neither was very interested in religion, but both loved England. When the archbishop of Canterbury died, Henry saw an opportunity and made Thomas the next archbishop. Thomas took his position seriously, deepening his prayer life and becoming a faithful priest. He soon found himself in a hard spot. His former friend, the King, wanted him to support laws that would be bad for the Catholics of England. Thomas knew he could not betray his people that way, which frustrated the King. A few days after Christmas, knights in the King's service stormed into the cathedral and killed Thomas while he was praying.

St. Patrick   DATES: ca. 389–ca. 461 | FEAST: March 17

When Patrick was a boy, he was captured by slave traders and taken to Ireland. There he spent six years as a shepherd. He had lots of time for prayer and learned to talk to God as a friend. One day in a vision, God showed him a way to escape. Back home, Patrick became a priest. However, he had a love for the people of Ireland and was sad because they did not know Jesus. In another vision, God asked him to go back to Ireland to preach the Gospel. The Irish were won over by Patrick's preaching and his fatherly love for them. Over half the people in Ireland converted because of him.

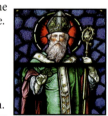

St. Josaphat   DATES: 1580–1623 | FEAST: November 12

Josaphat was an archbishop in Ukraine who was completely faithful to the Catholic Church. However, there were people in his diocese who were not loyal to the pope. Josaphat worked to unite them to the Church under the pope's authority. His goal was to bring his beloved country out of religious feuds to unity in the one true Church.

A mob attacked and killed Josaphat. His death was a shock to both sides in the conflict and brought a temporary peace to the area.

Prayer

Dear Jesus,

Please bless my country and all those who work hard to lead it. Thank You for blessing us with many good gifts! May You always be King of this land. May You be glorified through its government and laws. Give me a heart of service, especially toward those who are weak and defenseless.

LOVING WITH JUSTICE
RELATED VIRTUE OF JUSTICE
PRAYERFULNESS

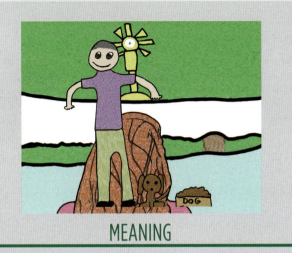

MEANING
Being still, listening, and being willing to talk to God as a friend

OPPOSING TRAIT
Entertaining distractions during prayers and Mass

WAYS TO CULTIVATE

AGES 6 AND UP — Fold your hands while you pray. "I love you, Jesus."

AGES 10 AND UP — Maintain a spirit of stillness with your body, mind, and heart while praying; make visits to the chapel; create a place of prayer in your home.

AGES 12 AND UP — Foster a spirit of interiority in your body, mind, and heart; participate in the sacraments regularly; make a place of prayer in your home.

Scripture

1 Kings 19:11–13	Matthew 11:25–27	John 15:23
Psalm 46:10–11	Mark 5:25–34	1 Corinthians 14:15
Psalm 141:2	Mark 6:31	Philippians 2:10–11
Ecclesiastes 3:7	Luke 2:36–38	Philippians 4:4–7
Matthew 2:9–11	Luke 24:28–32	1 Thessalonians 5:16–19
Matthew 6:6–15	John 4:7	James 5:13–15

SAINTS

St. Dominic   DATES: 1170–1221 | FEAST: August 8

It has been said that Dominic was always speaking about God or to God. He never had his own bed because he spent the night in the church praying. He would lie down on the steps to get a little sleep. Dominic's companions often saw him praying in many different postures. He would raise his arms in supplication, genuflect several times in front of the altar, or bow before a crucifix or statue of Jesus. His example of prayer made an impression on his followers. Soon after his death, the Dominicans wrote *The Nine Ways of Prayer of St. Dominic*.

St. Catherine of Siena   DATES: 1347–1380 | FEAST: April 29

Even as a little girl, Catherine had a deep love for God and wanted to give her whole life to Him. She would often go to her room and spend a long time in prayer. Her mother didn't understand this and made her do the servant's work so she would not have time to pray. Catherine did this cheerfully and was able to pray in her heart while doing the chores. Because of her constant union with God, He was able to use her to teach others, even the Pope.

St. Catherine is a doctor of the Church.

Bl. Elizabeth of the Trinity   DATES: 1880–1906 | FEAST: November 6

Elizabeth started out as a strong-willed, stubborn child, but she had a great desire to enter the Carmelite monastery in Dijon, France. When she was twenty-one she became a Carmelite, and she found great joy in praying before Jesus in the tabernacle and thinking about the Blessed Trinity. She said that her name in heaven would be *Laudem Gloriae*, "Praise of Glory," for she desired to praise God's glory eternally in whatever way He desired.

St. Hildegard of Bingen   DATES: 1098–1179 | FEAST: September 17

By the time she was eight years old, Hildegard of Bingen knew that she would become a religious sister. God spoke to her in visions, and she learned much from Him about the Scriptures and the history of salvation. Because of her many hours speaking with and listening to God, Hildegard was able to teach others about His plan. She wrote many letters, poems, and songs to describe the beauty of God and His creation.

Prayer

Dear Jesus,

I desire to have You as my best friend. Give me a desire to spend time with You each day, as I do with my friends. Help me always to put You first in my life, even when I am busy.

LOVING WITH JUSTICE

RELATED VIRTUE OF JUSTICE

RESPECT

JUSTICE

MEANING

Speaking and acting according to our own and others' rights, status, and circumstances

OPPOSING TRAIT

Resisting the directives of rightful authority

WAYS TO CULTIVATE

AGES 6 AND UP — Listen and smile when asked to do something. "Yes, Mom." "Excuse me, Dad." "Yes, Sister."

AGES 10 AND UP — Be respectful in words and actions toward people, places, and things.

AGES 12 AND UP — Be respectful in words and actions toward people, places, and things; avoid sarcasm.

Scripture

Genesis 41:46–49, 53–57
Exodus 20:1–17
Deuteronomy 6:4–9
Psalm 138:1–2
Luke 2:51–52
Romans 5:12
Romans 14:10, 12
Romans 14:15–16
Galatians 6:4–5
Colossians 3:23–24

SAINTS

Bl. Anna Maria Taigi   DATES: 1769–1837 | FEAST: June 9

Anna Maria lived in Italy and married a hot-tempered man. She never responded in anger to his harsh outbursts, but chose to respect him by replying gently and with a smile. Her respect toward her husband eventually calmed his temper and helped him become a more courteous person.

St. Damien of Molokai   DATES: 1840–1889 | FEAST: May 10

Fr. Damien was a Belgian missionary priest serving in Hawaii when he heard about the leper colony on the island of Molokai. People treated the lepers like outcasts, forcing them to live on the island without care or enough food or clothing. Damien wanted to take care of the lepers to show them their dignity as children of God. He spent the rest of his life serving these very sick people.

St. Frances of Rome   DATES: 1384–1440 | FEAST: March 9

Frances was born in Rome in 1384. As a young woman she married a man named Lorenzo and had three sons. At that time in Rome, several epidemics of plague broke out in the city. Sometimes the sick were abandoned because there were not enough people to care for them. Frances would walk the streets of Rome looking for the sick. She brought them home and cared for them there. When her house was full she would visit the hospitals so the sick there would not feel lonely. After her husband's death, she founded an order of sisters to care for the sick.

St. Catherine of Alexandria   DATES: 282–305 | FEAST: November 25

In the ancient world, Alexandria was the city with the best schools and wisest teachers. By the age of eighteen, Catherine was well-known for her wisdom and goodness, even though she was a Christian. The ruler of the city wanted her to commit a sin and give up her Christian faith. She respectfully refused. He brought several of his wisest teachers to talk her out of her faith. Catherine answered all their objections and was able to explain the faith calmly. The ruler grew angry as Catherine was speaking and he ordered her to be put to death.

Prayer

Dear Jesus,

Help me to show reverence to people who are in authority over me as I would to You. And help me give all persons the honor they deserve as Your unique creations.

LOVING WITH JUSTICE
RELATED VIRTUE OF JUSTICE
RESPONSIBILITY

MEANING

Fulfilling our just duties; accepting the consequences of one's words and actions, intentional and unintentional

OPPOSING TRAIT

Failing to accept responsibility for one's words and/or actions; being unreliable

WAYS TO CULTIVATE

AGES 6 AND UP	Complete your tasks. "I have finished my homework."
AGES 10 AND UP	Be responsible for your homework, duties, etc.; admit when you are wrong or when you have done something wrong.
AGES 12 AND UP	Be accountable for decisions and actions at home, at school, and in personal relationships.

Scripture

Genesis 29:1–3

Genesis 41:46–49, 53–57

Psalm 128:1–2

Luke 2:51–52

Acts 10:17–33

2 Corinthians 7:1

Colossians 3:23–24

SAINTS

St. Margaret of Scotland   DATES: 1045–1092 | FEAST: November 16

Margaret was an English princess who met her future husband in an unusual way. She was traveling by sea when a violent storm wrecked their boat off the coast of Scotland, near the king's castle. She met the king, and they married. As queen of Scotland she had many responsibilities. She was careful to take care of the poor and made sure that the people were able to go to Mass. She reformed the laws and courts so they were fair and just.

St. Lawrence   DATES: Died 258 | FEAST: August 10

Lawrence lived in Rome during the persecution of Valerian. He was a deacon and worked closely with Pope St. Sixtus II. As a deacon, it was his job to take care of the Church's money. His most important task was to help the poor, especially the widows and orphans. The Romans heard that Lawrence was the Church's treasurer. They ordered him to hand over the treasures of the Church, thinking they would get gold and silver. Instead he brought the poor of Rome and said they were the Church's true treasure. St. Lawrence and Pope Sixtus were martyred a few days apart.

St. Pius V   DATES: 1504–1572 | FEAST: April 30

The last great naval battle against the Turks was the Battle of Lepanto in 1571. If the Christians lost, the Muslims would begin their conquest of Europe.

Pope Pius V called all Christians in Rome to pray the Rosary, asking Our Lady to grant the Christians victory. Catholics already loved and trusted Pius V because he had made sweeping reforms in the Vatican, simplifying and reorganizing the life of the Church. They prayed the Rosary as he asked, and their prayers to the Mother of God brought victory to the Christian military and saved Europe.

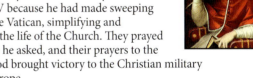

St. Columba   DATES: 521–597 | FEAST: June 9

Columba was born in Ireland in the sixth century. He went to school at a monastery and soon became one of their best writers. Monastery schools were just beginning in Ireland and Columba worked hard to copy books for the students. In 563, he and twelve companions left Ireland for Scotland to preach. They told the Scots about the Gospel and built monasteries and schools. Columba traveled all over Ireland and Scotland until he was an old man. When he was too old to travel, visitors would come to his cell. They often found him copying books for the schools, just as he had done as a young monk.

Prayer

Dear Jesus,

Please help me to be faithful in all the duties You have entrusted to me this day, fulfilling each with great care and love!

LOVING WITH JUSTICE

RELATED VIRTUE OF JUSTICE

SINCERITY

MEANING

Trustfulness in words and actions; honesty and enthusiasm toward others

OPPOSING TRAIT

Speaking or acting in a manner only to make oneself look good; being insincere

WAYS TO CULTIVATE

AGES 6 AND UP — Pay attention when others are speaking. "May I help you?"

AGES 10 AND UP — Speak and act honestly.

AGES 12 AND UP — Say what you mean; build trust by your words and actions; state when you are sorry and what you are grateful for.

Scripture

2 Corinthians 8:8	Mark 14:3–9	Romans 12:9
Psalm 27:1–4	Luke 16:10	1 Timothy 1:5
Matthew 5:33–37	Luke 19:8–10	Colossians 3:23
Matthew 6:5–6	Acts 4:18–20	1 John 3:18

SAINTS

St. Peter Claver DATES: 1581–1654 | FEAST: September 9

There was an active slave trade in Latin America when Peter arrived there from Spain in 1610. Calling himself the "slave of slaves," Peter would meet each slave ship as it arrived so he could provide the slaves with food and medicine. He expressed his sincere love by trying to help each person with his immediate needs and then telling him or her about the love of Jesus.

Peter strove to help all retain their human dignity. His sincerity melted the slaves' hearts, and many were converted to Christianity.

St. Anthony of Padua DATES: 1195–1231 | FEAST: June 13

Anthony was born in Lisbon, Portugal, to a wealthy family. When he was a young man, God called him to give up his wealth to join the new Franciscan order. He was ordained a priest and was a great preacher. People loved to listen to him because of his sincerity and gentleness. Once while visiting a town to preach there, Anthony spent the night at a man's home. The man was astonished when he walked into Anthony's room. Anthony was praying and holding the child Jesus, who was surrounded with a heavenly light. This is why many images of St. Anthony show him with the child Jesus.

St. Vincent Ferrer DATES: 1350–1419 | FEAST: April 5

Vincent Ferrer, a Dominican friar, loved the people to whom he preached. He was so concerned about the sincerity of their relationship with God that he was not afraid to tell them boldly about the evil of sin. Because they knew of his kindness and sincere interest in their souls, many heeded Fr. Vincent's warnings, converted, and lived holy lives.

St. Augustine of Canterbury DATES: Died ca. 604 | FEAST: May 27

Pope Gregory the Great asked Augustine, a monk, to take thirty missionaries and evangelize England, a pagan country. When they reached England, they were afraid because they could not speak the language. Yet Augustine and his men worked hard to teach the natives to trust them: they learned English customs and the language, removed pagan idols without destroying the temples, and lived simple, sincere Christian lives.

Prayer

Dear Jesus,

Please give me the grace to be honest in all my words and actions. When someone is speaking, give me the patience to listen attentively.

LOVING WITH JUSTICE
RELATED VIRTUE OF JUSTICE: TRUSTWORTHINESS

MEANING
Acting in a way that inspires confidence and trust; being reliable

OPPOSING TRAIT
Being devious or deceptive

WAYS TO CULTIVATE

AGES 6 AND UP — Tell the truth. "I will take the money to the office."

AGES 10 AND UP — Do the right thing even when no one is watching.

AGES 12 AND UP — Be faithful in small matters.

Scripture

2 Samuel 7:28–29	Zechariah 8:16–17	Luke 8:47
2 Corinthians 13:5	Matthew 24:45–47	Luke 16:10
Psalm 25:21	Matthew 28:507	1 Corinthians 4:1–2
Proverbs 28:6	Luke 1:36	Ephesians 4:29–31

SAINTS

Bl. Anne-Marie Javouhey
DATES: 1779–1851 | **FEAST:** July 15

Anne-Marie grew up in a Catholic family while the French Revolution was trying to destroy the Catholic Faith. Anne-Marie had a deep love for Jesus and felt Him calling her to be a religious sister, but there were no more convents in France. She founded a religious community of sisters to run free schools for poor children. By 1804, there was a new government, and while it did not trust the Catholics, it allowed Anne-Marie to open schools. Years later, the government decided to free six hundred slaves in French Africa. They wanted someone to teach the newly freed people to be safe and able to take care of themselves. The government recognized that Anne-Marie was a trustworthy teacher and asked her to teach them. The Africans in French Guiana loved her, and were grateful for her help.

St. Tarcisius
DATES: Early Third Century | **FEAST:** August 15

Tarcisius was a boy in Rome when Christians had to meet secretly for Mass. One day, the pope needed someone to carry the Eucharist to another place. Tarcisius volunteered, saying that no one would suspect a boy. The pope finally agreed, and Tarcisius was overjoyed. As he walked, Tarcisius prayed to Jesus as he held Him in his hands. In a field he met some mean boys who began to taunt him, trying to pull his hands away, but his arms could not be moved. One of them said, "He must be a Christian," and they began to beat and kick him. The boys ran off when a Christian soldier walked by. He carried Tarcisius to the pope; only then did his arms loosen so the pope could take the Eucharist. He faithfully defended the Eucharist with his life.

St. Bernard
DATES: 1090–1153 | **FEAST:** August 20

Bernard was born into a noble French family that loved their Catholic faith. After they death of his saintly mother, Bernard entered the Cistercian monastery. Several of his brothers and friends loved and trusted him, so they too entered the monastery. As the years went on, even popes and kings asked the trustworthy Bernard for advice. He has been declared a Doctor of the Church because we can trust that what he wrote about God and the Blessed Mother is true.

St. Agnes of Montepulciano
DATES: 1268–1317 | **FEAST:** April 20

When she was only nine years old, Agnes asked her parents to let her enter the convent at Montepulciano. They hesitated, but knowing that Agnes was a mature and devout child, they agreed to let her enter. When she was fourteen the sisters put her in charge of procuring all the food, clothing, and other needs of the community. The next year the pope himself asked her to become superior of a new community and teach its sisters.

Prayer
Dear Jesus,
Help me to be faithful in even the little things of each day. In Your eyes nothing is little when done with great love!

CONTENDING WITH FORTITUDE

FORTITUDE

Fortitude can be represented by a shield, for it is the virtue of strength. It enables one to persevere in the pursuit of goodness in the face of difficulties, even to the point of sacrifice. Christian fortitude recognizes that God is our highest good and guards one's relationship with God, even if martyrdom should be the cost.

"What will separate us from the love of Christ? Will anguish, or distress, or persecution, or famine, or nakedness, or peril, or the sword? As it is written: 'For your sake we are being slain all the day; we are looked upon as sheep to be slaughtered.'"

—Romans 8:35-37

RELATED VIRTUES:

INDUSTRIOUSNESS MAGNANIMITY MAGNIFICENCE PATIENCE

PERSEVERANCE

FORTITUDE

KNOW IT

 CONTENDING WITH FORTITUDE

Cardinal Virtue of Fortitude

CCC, 1808
CCC, 1837

Summa Theologiae

II–II.Q123–140, St. Thomas Aquinas

Echoing the Mystery

50-Cardinal Virtue of Fortitude

FORTITUDE enables one to endure difficulties and pain for the sake of what is good.

Fortitude is the cardinal virtue that perfects our emotions, particularly by freeing us from the grip of fear and anger. It makes us strong in the pursuit of goodness, helping us to resist temptations and overcome obstacles. When inspired by charity, it empowers us to hope in Christ's strength to make us confident and even joyful in the face of trials, persecution, and even death. Christian martyrdom is a shining example of fortitude.

 Key Points
- Aims to perfect our emotions in face of difficult situations
- Strengthens the will in the pursuit of the good
- Overcomes fear and moderates anger in the face of trials

GUARD IT

The cardinal virtue of fortitude aims to strengthen us in the pursuit of good despite difficulties. At our Baptism, our heavenly Father gave us this virtue to strengthen us, particularly in the face of human weakness, fears, and temptations.

The following are some sins against fortitude:

Sins Against Fortitude		
Cowardice	Fearlessness or Recklessness	Sloth or Acedia
Unwilling to withstand the difficulties that are inherent in doing the good	Thoughtlessly dismissing as unimportant dangers that ought to be prudently avoided	Inability to make decisions because the lost desire for the good
Example: Remaining quiet when you should defend someone	*Example*: Engaging in dangerous recreation	*Example*: The thought of practicing virtue causes dread and immobility

FORTITUDE

GUARD IT

The virtues related to fortitude strengthen us in living the Christian life. Guarding ourselves from these sins will enable us to remain firm and constant in the pursuit of good.

RELATED VIRTUES	MEANING	OPPOSING VICE
Magnanimity	Seeking with confidence to do great things in God; literally "having a large soul"	**Presumption:** relying only oneself in attempting projects or actions beyond one's ability **Ambition:** seeking honors based on one's merit or state **Vainglory:** unduly seeking fame and popularity without proper credit given to God **Pusillanimity (faintheartedness):** unreasonable lack of confidence—false humility—which prevents one from using his God-given talents
Magnificence	Doing great things for God; willingness to spend one's resources to accomplish the work	**Mediocrity:** withholding what is necessary to get a job done **Wastefulness:** spending beyond what is required
Patience	Bearing present difficulties calmly	**Impatience:** excessive need to defend oneself or to protect oneself against all discomfort—externally manifested by anger, complaints, and murmuring; internally by a feeling of dislike toward any trial or suffering **Insensibility or hardness of heart:** remaining stoically unmoved and insensible in the face of suffering
Longanimity	Striving for some good that is a long way off	**Inconstancy:** giving up the practice of virtue as soon as difficulties and obstacles arise (fickleness) **Pertinacity:** obstinacy and unwillingness to yield when right reason requires it; being opinionated and headstrong
Perseverance	Taking the steps necessary to carry out objectives in spite of difficulties	
Constancy	Strength of soul against the difficulties that proceed from obstacles	

> Sometimes it is much harder to look every day at disappointment, dashed hopes, betrayal, failures, and hopelessness than it is to look down the barrel of a gun. Sometimes the greatest test of courage is in the face of terminal illness. If we ask for the gift of courage, we will receive it.
> —Fr. Benedict Groeschel, The Virtue Driven Life

> For Mary there were many struggles ahead, as she lived out the consequences of the "yes" that she had given to the Lord… Throughout her trials she remained faithful to her promise, sustained by the Spirit of fortitude.
> —Pope Benedict XVI, Angelus, July 20, 2008

> "I have told you this so that you might have peace in me. In the world you will have trouble, but take courage, I have conquered the world."
> —John 16:33

FORTITUDE

GUARD IT

RELATED BEATITUDE

The Gift of Fortitude

"Blessed are they who hunger and thirst for righteousness." —Matthew 5:6

The gift of fortitude fills us with a confidence which empowers us to counter evil and persevere in doing good. It is the gift that supports man's longing for righteousness.

Summa Theologiae

II–II.Q139, St. Thomas Aquinas

Fortitude moves one to endure difficulties for the sake of eternal life with God.

The cardinal virtue of fortitude strengthens the will in the pursuit of the good. The distinguishing mark of the **Gift of Fortitude** is confidence amidst the faithful and heroic performance of one's responsibilities, great or small. In the face of sudden temptation, the Holy Spirit's gift of fortitude gives the disciple strength to overcome the temptation and choose heroic virtue.

Effects of the Gift of the Holy Spirit

- Certain, unshakable confidence in God, particularly in the face of sorrows or misfortunes
- Victory over lukewarmness, sloth, or laziness
- Fidelity to one's responsibilities, including enduring patiently the trials of everyday life
- Ability to withstand temptation and pressure toward sin
- Joy, even in the midst of suffering and pain

Vice That Opposes the Gift of Fortitude:

Sloth or **acedia** is culpable for lack of physical and spiritual effort.

"The spiritual writers understand by this vice (acedia) as a form of depression due to lax ascetical practice, decreasing vigilance or carelessness of heart. 'The spirit indeed is willing, but the flesh is weak'" (*CCC*, 2733). *See Acedia Chart on page 45.*

PRAY IT *LECTIO DIVINA*

Luke 12:1–9

Meanwhile, so many people were crowding together that they were trampling one another underfoot. He began to speak, first to his disciples, "Beware of the leaven—that is, the hypocrisy—of the Pharisees. There is nothing concealed that will not be revealed, nor secret that will not be known. Therefore whatever you have said in the darkness will be heard in the light, and what you have whispered behind closed doors will be proclaimed on the housetops. I tell you, my friends, do not be afraid of those who kill the body but after that can do no more. I shall show you whom to fear. Be afraid of the one who after killing has the  *power to cast into Gehenna; yes, I tell you, be afraid of that one. Are not five sparrows sold for two small coins? Yet not one of them has escaped the notice of God. Even the hairs of your head have all been counted. Do not be afraid. You are worth more than many sparrows. I tell you, everyone who acknowledges me before others the Son of Man will acknowledge before the angels of God. But whoever denies me before others will be denied before the angels of God."*

1. God's Word strikes the heart. What word or phrase touched your heart?
2. Jesus warned the crowds about the leaven of the Pharisees. Why was this warning necessary? Think about how leaven affects the dough.
3. Who did Jesus say we must fear and why?
4. What did Jesus reveal to us about the Father's love? How does this bring you comfort?
5. Ask this question in prayer: "Jesus, show me how I can daily acknowledge You before others. How can I live as an authentic and sincere disciple?" Write down what you hear Him saying to you.

Pray an Act of Fortitude

Dear Jesus,

*Alone I am weak, but with You I can do all things.
Give me the grace to be strong against temptations and
bold in proclaiming You and Your Church on earth.*

FORTITUDE

LIVE IT LOOKING TO THE SAINTS

BL. CHIARA LUCE BADANO

If you look at a photograph of Blessed Chiara Luce, she looks like the girl next door. She has a wide grin, a striped shirt, and her tousled hair pushed back from her face. She was born in 1971 in a small town in Italy. She was an only child, born after her parents had struggled with infertility for eleven years. Her parents had a strong and lively faith, and Chiara enjoyed participating in youth groups and retreats. There her faith was nourished and strengthened.

> **Contending with Fortitude**
>
> She would say that her heart was singing, even in the midst of her suffering, because she was able to offer everything to Jesus.

Chiara did nothing extraordinary. She went to school and hung out with her friends. She liked singing, swimming, and tennis. Once, when she was little, her mother asked her to clear the table. She refused and left the room. A little later, she came back in. She told her mother that she been thinking about the parable of the man who asked his two sons to do something. One said he would, but went away and did something else. The other refused, but later came back and was obedient (Matthew 28:28–31). She wanted to be obedient, and asked her mother if she would help her put her apron on.

But Chiara's life was marked by extraordinary faith. When she was nine, her family went to a Focolare "Family Fest." There, the Gospels came alive for her in a new way, and she wrote to Chiara Lubich, "Now I want this book to be the sole purpose of my life." She began to consciously offer everything to Jesus. She also tried to share the Gospel with her friends. She did it primarily by the witness of her example and by her love.

When Chiara was seventeen, she felt a stabbing pain in her shoulder while playing tennis. She was soon diagnosed with osteosarcoma, an aggressive bone cancer. It was hard news for a teenager who loved life and being active. After her first treatment her mother tried to talk to her about it. Chiara threw herself on her bed, refusing to look at her mother. A while later, she was able to smile and tell her mother, "Mom, you can talk to me now." Saying "yes" to Jesus was a struggle, and yet in that "yes" Chiara Luce became a shining witness to joy.

Doctors, priests, and even a cardinal came to visit Chiara after hearing about her joy in the midst of suffering. She would say that her heart was singing, even in the midst of her suffering, because she was able to offer everything to Jesus. One doctor said, "Through her smile, and through her eyes full of light, she showed us that death doesn't exist; only life exists." When a cardinal asked her where the light in her eyes came from, she said, "I try to love Jesus as much as I can." Her pain was excruciating and yet she refused morphine because "it takes away my lucidity" and "I can only offer my pain to Jesus. It's all I have left." As each lock of hair fell out, she said "for You, Jesus" each time.

Chiara requested to be buried in a wedding gown since it would be the day that she saw Jesus. She died on October 7, 1990 surrounded by family and friends. Her last words were, "Goodbye. Be happy because I'm happy." As she watched her death approach, she told others that she felt "enfolded in a marvelous plan of God." This reality gave her confidence and courage in the face of her sufferings.

LIVE IT

FORTITUDE

FORTITUDE moves one to endure difficulties for the sake of eternal life with God.

A Disciple of Christ living the virtue of fortitude…

- ✓ Shows firmness in difficulties
- ✓ Is constant in the pursuit of good
- ✓ Moderates the emotions of anger and fear which come into play when a person faces a complex and difficult situation
- ✓ Does not engage in gossip or participate in unjust acts

Fortitude (courage) enables one to endure difficulties for what is good. This virtue aids us in everyday situations to live prudently, justly, and temperately.

In the words of St. Pope John Paul II…

There are many, a great many manifestations of fortitude, often heroic, of which nothing is written in the newspapers, or of which little is known. Only human conscience knows them…and God knows!

I wish to pay tribute to all these unknown courageous people. To all those who have the courage to say "no" or "yes," when they have to pay a price to do so! To the men who bear an extraordinary witness to human dignity and deep humanity. Just because they are unknown, they deserve a tribute and special recognition. —St. Pope John Paul II, General Audience, Wednesday, 15 November 1978

Going Deeper in Fortitude

FROM THE CATECHISM

Fortitude ensures firmness in difficulties and constancy in the pursuit of the good (*CCC*, 1837).

Fortitude strengthens the resolve to resist temptations and to overcome obstacles in the moral life. The virtue of fortitude enables one to conquer fear, even fear of death, and to face trials and persecutions. It disposes one even to renounce and sacrifice his life in defense of a just cause. "The Lord is my strength and my song" [Psalm 118:14]. "In the world you have tribulation; but be of good cheer, I have overcome the world" [John 16:33] (*CCC*, 1808).

Christian Martyrdom

"Once again, where does the strength to face martyrdom come from? From deep and intimate union with Christ, because martyrdom and the vocation to martyrdom are not the result of human effort but the response to a project and call of God, they are a gift of his grace that enables a person, out of love, to give his life for Christ and for the Church, hence for the world. If we read the lives of the Martyrs we are amazed at their calmness and courage in confronting suffering and death: God's power is fully expressed in weakness, in the poverty of those who entrust themselves to him and place their hope in him alone (see also 2 Corinthians 12:9). Yet it is important to stress that God's grace does not suppress or suffocate the freedom of those who face martyrdom; on the contrary it enriches and exalts them: the Martyr is an exceedingly free person, free as regards power, as regards the world; a free person who in a single, definitive act gives God his whole life, and in a supreme act of faith, hope and charity, abandons himself into the hands of his Creator and Redeemer; he gives up his life in order to be associated totally with the Sacrifice of Christ on the Cross. In a word, martyrdom is a great act of love in response to God's immense love." —Pope Benedict XVI, *General Audience*, August 2, 2010

The Blessed Virgin Mary and the Gifts of the Holy Spirit

The Finding in the Temple and the Gift of Fortitude

What kind of terror must have seized the hearts of Mary and Joseph when they discovered their child missing from the traveling party on their journey home from the Passover feast in Jerusalem (Luke 2:41–45)? How did they console and fortify themselves as they urgently retraced their steps back to the place where they had last seen their twelve year old son? They must have been encouraged with the Holy Spirit's Gift of Fortitude.

The Gift of Fortitude or courage is a kind of firmness of mind needed for doing good and enduring evil. This gift surpasses the natural moral virtue of courage by its power to make us confident of escaping each and every danger, even those that make steadfastness outstandingly difficult. That was the kind of situation Mary and Joseph faced. The Gift of Fortitude empowered them to repulse the frightful imaginings and scenarios that must have tormented their minds as they searched sorrowfully for Jesus (cf. Luke 2:48).

The chief act of the Gift of Fortitude is to enable us to stand our ground amidst dangers. In this way, the Gift prevented Mary and Joseph from jumping to false conclusions about why their child was missing. For through this Gift, the Holy Spirit moves the human mind in a way that surpasses what is natural and peculiar to it so as to reach the end of a good work begun. Simeon a few years earlier had revealed to Joseph and Mary the divine work that had begun in Jesus: "This child is destined to be the downfall and rise of many" (Luke 2:34). Therefore, the Holy Spirit fortified them through his special Gift to remain steadfast in their confidence despite the many excruciating anxieties and nightmares that must have plagued them.

Mary and Joseph sought their lost son like a parched man seeking water. St. Augustine says that courage befits those who thirst because they work hard to achieve the joy that springs from the good thing they seek. The fruits of the Gift of Fortitude are eminent in Mary and Joseph. They manifest a holy patience that enables them to endure the evil of being separated from their son. And they demonstrate long-suffering: that forbearance to wait in perseverance and faith all the while performing the good works necessary to restore their tranquility and peace.

In God's providence, it is necessary for Mary to suffer this grueling experience. For it prepares the Blessed Mother for that other excruciating experience of the cross. It is on Calvary that Mary's sanctified courage is truly displayed. Yet, this experience of losing her Son in its own way is a foreshadowing and prefigurement of the Passion and death of Jesus. "On the third day" Joseph and Mary find Jesus in the temple. And on the third day the Risen Jesus appears to his believers. Mary's finding of the child Jesus is like a mini-Resurrection in advance. But before the real thing, Mary—and we—must be fortified with the Spirit's Gift of Fortitude so that we have the perseverance to stand firm and face death in our life, in whatever form it may come.

Just as courage led the Blessed Virgin Mary to Jesus, so too will our union with Mary in the Spirit's Gift of Fortitude lead us to eternal life with Jesus.

"Finding in the Temple and the Gift of Fortitude," pg. 36. Cameron, Peter John O.P. *The Gifts of the Holy Spirit.* Veritas Series. Connecticut: Knights of Columbus, 2002.

CONTENDING WITH FORTITUDE

RELATED VIRTUE OF FORTITUDE

INDUSTRIOUSNESS

MEANING

Diligence, especially in work that leads to natural and supernatural maturity

OPPOSING TRAIT

Giving in to a lack of motivation to complete one's responsibilities; being lazy

WAYS TO CULTIVATE

AGES 6 AND UP — Work to complete your duties. "Let me finish this first."

AGES 10 AND UP — Diligently complete a task; set small goals along the way.

AGES 12 AND UP — Work diligently, especially in things that lead to natural and supernatural maturity.

Scripture

Genesis 2:3	Proverbs 20:13	Luke 6:6–19
Nehemiah 4:15–17	Proverbs 28:19	Colossians 3:23–24
Psalm 90:17	Proverbs 31:10–31	1 Thessalonians 2:9
Proverbs 6:10–12	Jeremiah 29:11	Romans 12:11
Proverbs 10:4	Matthew 4:23	Titus 2:7–8
Proverbs 12:24	Luke 5:18–19	

FORTITUDE

SAINTS

St. Cyril — DATES: ca. 825–869 | FEAST: February 14
St. Methodius — DATES: ca. 826–884

Cyril and Methodius were brothers who grew up in Greece. Cyril became a priest and Methodius a monk, and both were sent to Russia as missionaries. The inhabitants of Russia in the ninth century did not have a written language, so it was difficult to teach them Scripture or the *Catechism*. Cyril and Methodius worked together to learn the many varieties of the Slavonic languages, create an alphabet, and translate the Scriptures. They worked hard to preach the Gospel and celebrate the sacraments in ways that the people would understand.

St. Bede — DATES: ca. 673–735 | FEAST: MAY 25

Bede was an English monk in the early Middle Ages. At that time there were not very many books because they were so large and were written by hand. Bede worked in the monastery's scriptorium, the room where the monks copied books. He would meditate on the Scripture passages as he copied them. Soon he was writing his own books. Most were about Scripture, but he also wrote about history and philosophy. He wrote the first history of England and Ireland. He died when he was sixty-two and had written forty-five books.

St. John Neumann — DATES: 1811–1860 | FEAST: January 5

John was born in what is now the Czech Republic and sailed to America as a young man. He became a Redemptorist priest and eventually became the fourth bishop of Philadelphia. Bishop Neumann started one hundred Catholic schools in eight years, wrote catechisms and other pamphlets to teach the faith, and worked to bring good teachers into the diocese. He traveled across his diocese even though the roads were bad. He learned Gaelic so he could preach to the Irish immigrants. His life's work was to spread the faith.

St. Anthony Mary Claret — DATES: 1807–1870 | FEAST: October 24

Anthony Claret was born in Barcelona, Spain. He was the archbishop of Santiago, Cuba. He realized that if his parishioners did not read good books, they would choose books that turned them away from God. He began printing pamphlets and booklets for them about the faith. Realizing success in this, he worked diligently to write and print over one hundred books about the Catholic faith.

Prayer

Heavenly Father,
You have given me the gift of this day, the gift of this moment. Help me to use my time well. Give me the grace to do all for Your greater glory.

CONTENDING WITH FORTITUDE

RELATED VIRTUE OF FORTITUDE
MAGNANIMITY

MEANING

Seeking with confidence to do great things in God; literally "having a large soul"

OPPOSING TRAIT

Seeking to do great things for self-promotion—also not seeking to do the good that is possible—pusillanimity (weak, spineless)

WAYS TO CULTIVATE

AGES 6 AND UP — Compliment someone else when you want to be recognized. "You did a great job."

AGES 10 AND UP — Allow others to receive the praise and credit they deserve; ask God to help you recognize the good in others.

AGES 12 AND UP — Acknowledge the good in others when it is difficult; strive to do difficult tasks with God's grace.

Scripture

1 Samuel 17:25–26, 32–47	1 Corinthians 9:16–23	Colossians 1:28–29
Esther 13:13–17	1 Corinthians 15:10	
Matthew 28:16–20	2 Corinthians 12:15	
Luke 1:38	Ephesians 6:10–11	
Acts 9:17–22	Philippians 4:13	

SAINTS

St. Philip Neri
DATES: 1515–1595 | **FEAST:** May 26

In sixteenth-century Rome many people, even some leaders in the Church were falling away from God. Philip devoted his life to bringing all he could persuade back to the true Church. He used jokes, discussions, and even popular songs to show others that the Church is a joyful place. Though the task of converting the city seemed impossible for one man, Philip Neri trusted that God would use him to do great things for the Church.

St. Louis de Montfort
DATES: 1673–1716 | **FEAST:** April 28

Louis was born to a very devout family in France. Early on he decided that he wanted to become a priest. His friendships and prayer life led him to a deep and intimate love of the Blessed Virgin Mary.

As a missionary, Louis traveled anywhere and everywhere to bring the love of Mother Mary to people. He wrote several books, including *The Secret of the Rosary* and *True Devotion to Mary*. His teachings have endured, and they inspired a young Karol Wojtyla—the future St. Pope John Paul II—to entrust his entire life "to Jesus through Mary."

St. Paul Miki
DATES: ca. 1564–1597 | **FEAST:** February 6

Paul, a young Japanese convert to Christianity, entered the seminary to become a Jesuit. The Japanese government was persecuting Christians at this time, and Paul was captured and sentenced to death. He prayed that God would forgive his captors, and he said to those standing nearby at his crucifixion, "Ask Christ to help you become happy."

St. Turibius of Mongrovejo
DATES: 1538–1606 | **FEAST:** March 23

Turibius was a law professor in Spain when the pope unexpectedly named him the archbishop of Lima, Peru. Turibius had not even been ordained a priest yet!

When Bishop Turibius went to Peru, he discovered poverty and lack of education throughout the country. He determined to right this, and over the next seven years he visited every parish in his diocese, traveling alone over thousands of miles of jungle territory. He led a reform among the priests, printed catechisms in the natives' language, and made the sacraments available to all in his diocese.

Prayer

Sacred Heart of Jesus,

You loved us even to the point of death. Give me a big heart! Give me Your heart! Help me to love others with all my heart!

FORTITUDE

CONTENDING WITH FORTITUDE

RELATED VIRTUE OF FORTITUDE

MAGNIFICENCE

MEANING
Doing great things for God

OPPOSING TRAIT
Being wasteful; not responding to grace

WAYS TO CULTIVATE

AGES 6 AND UP — Share; help others when you are good at something and they are not. "May I help you?"

AGES 10 AND UP — Be generous with your time and offer to help others; share.

AGES 12 AND UP — Use your talents for the good without complaining; be generous with your time.

Scripture

Exodus 35:29	Acts 10:1–8	2 Corinthians 9:11–15
Psalm 8:2, 6–7	Acts 11:27–30	Colossians 3:23–24
Matthew 25:14–29	1 Corinthians 10:31	1 Timothy 4:10
Luke 8:1–3	1 Corinthians 12:4–11	Hebrews 12:2–3
Luke 19:8	2 Corinthians 8:2–7	1 Peter 4:10–11

SAINTS

St. Pope John Paul II
DATES: 1920–2005 | **FEAST:** October 22

Karol Wojtyla grew up in Poland and became a priest after his studies in an underground seminary during World War II. Fr. Wojtyla gave himself wholeheartedly to whatever he was assigned to do, be it academic work or canoe trips with the youth in his parish.

When he became pope in 1978, John Paul II continued to lead the Church with great magnificence and enthusiasm. He started World Youth Days, invited all to come into the Church, and did other great things in love and wisdom, with hard work and perseverance, undergirded by an intense prayer life. He said, "Do not be afraid! " over and over again and was a real inspiration to many people, Catholics and non Catholics alike.

St. Maximilian Kolbe
DATES: 1894–1941 | **FEAST:** August 14

Maximilian was a Franciscan friar during World War II who worked to protect Christians and Jews from the Nazis. In the concentration camp at Auschwitz, he secretly gave his fellow prisoners the sacraments. One day the Nazis singled out ten men to because three men had escaped from the camp. Fr. Kolbe heard one man plead for his life because he had a family and offered to take his place. Thrown with the nine others into a starvation bunker, he offered Mass and led the men in praise of God, encouraging them with the fact that they would soon see the face of God.

St. Genevieve
DATES: 422–ca. 500 | **FEAST:** January 3

Genevieve was a young consecrated virgin when Paris was being invaded by the Franks. They had surrounded the city hoping to starve the people into surrender. She led a fleet of small ships up the river to gather grain. They brought it back to Paris, where several women went around the besieged city giving bread to anyone in need. In this way, they had enough to eat until the Franks were defeated.

St. Alban
DATES: Third Century | **FEAST:** September 27

Alban was a pagan in England when a priest fleeing persecutors asked him for refuge. Alban was so impressed by the priest that he was baptized. He then took the priest's cloak and gave the priest his own clothes. When the pursuers arrived, they arrested Alban instead of the priest.

Prayer

Heavenly Father,

You have given me the gift of this day, the gift of this moment. Help me to use my time well. Give me the grace to do all for Your greater glory.

CONTENDING WITH FORTITUDE

RELATED VIRTUE OF FORTITUDE
PATIENCE

MEANING
Bearing present difficulties calmly

OPPOSING TRAIT
Being impatient while completing a difficult task or in handling challenging circumstances

WAYS TO CULTIVATE

AGES 6 AND UP — Wait your turn; do not get upset if things do not go your way. "I will not complain."

AGES 10 AND UP — Be a good listener and don't interrupt; wait your turn.

AGES 12 AND UP — Listen to others; wait for your turn; tolerate inconveniences and annoyances.

Scripture

Genesis 29:20–28	Romans 8:24–30	2 Timothy 4:16–17
Lamentation 3:25–27	1 Corinthians 13:4	Hebrews 11:13–16
Mark 10:46–52	2 Corinthians 12:9–10	James 5:7–8
Luke 15:11–24	Galatians 5:22–23	2 Peter 1:5–8
Romans 5:2–4	Philippians 4:11–13	Revelation 3:10

Prayer
Dear God,
Help me to wait without complaining, to see You in my neighbor, and to let Your grace enter this moment so that I may not lose my patience.

SAINTS

St. Teresa of Calcutta — DATES: 1910–1997 | FEAST: September 5

Mother Teresa was on a train in India when she heard God's call to serve the poorest of the poor. She obeyed him and founded the Missionaries of Charity. She and her sisters took care of the very sick and poor people in Calcutta, picking them up off the streets and giving them a clean bed to lie upon. She was always gentle and patient with those who were suffering, and she taught her sisters to do the same. After she died, the world found out that her joy was the fruit of her patient acceptance of suffering. After that time on the train, Teresa never heard God's voice again. In fact, she felt like He had abandoned her. She even accepted this with a smile and it opened her heart to show God's love to others.

St. Alphonsus Liguori — DATES: 1696–1787 | FEAST: August 1

Alphonsus was a young lawyer in Italy when he realized that there were not enough priests to preach to the poor. He became a priest and started an order to preach in poor cities and villages. He was very good at helping people with difficult decisions. He was a patient listener and wrote a book to help priests be good confessors and spiritual guides. Alphonsus suffered through many struggles. Heretics tried to mislead the people he was teaching, and even the priests in his order turned against him and forced him to resign. He never complained and was admired for his gentleness and patience.

St. Gianna Molla — DATES: 1922–1962 | FEAST: April 28

Gianna was an Italian doctor and mother. She loved her husband very much, but he had to travel a lot for work. When he was away they often wrote letters when they could not talk on the telephone. She was honest about what was hard but was never bitter or angry. When she was pregnant with her fourth child, the doctors told her she needed surgery to save her life. She waited as long as she could and then chose the surgery that would be safest for her unborn child. The sacrifice she made for her baby cost Gianna her life.

St. Athanasius — DATES: ca. 295–373 | FEAST: May 2

As bishop of Alexandria, Athanasius knew that he had to protect his flock from the heresies of the Arians, who believed that Jesus was not truly God. He was hated and derided for adhering to the teachings of the Church and was even accused of crimes he had never committed. He was exiled from his city many times.

Athanasius never stopped teaching the truth, and eventually he was able to remain in Alexandria.

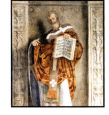

FORTITUDE

CONTENDING WITH FORTITUDE

RELATED VIRTUE OF FORTITUDE

PERSEVERANCE

MEANING

Taking the steps necessary to carry out objectives in spite of difficulties

OPPOSING TRAIT

Quickly giving up when a task is challenging

WAYS TO CULTIVATE

AGES 6 AND UP — Finish your chores and homework even when you don't feel like it; stay kneeling at Mass when required. "I am not going to give up!"

AGES 10 AND UP — Complete homework on time; finish chores even if bored or tired.

AGES 12 AND UP — Complete task from start to finish; stay with a task when it is hard, difficult, or boring.

Scripture

2 Maccabees 7:1–42	Galatians 6:9–10	Hebrews 12:11
Matthew 15:22–28	2 Corinthians 11:21–29	James 1:2–4
Mark 10:46–52	Colossians 1:11–12	James 1:12
Luke 11:5–13	2 Thessalonians 3:13	Revelation 2:10
John 14:15	Hebrews 10:36–39	Revelation 3:10
Romans 12:12	Hebrews 12:1–2	

SAINTS

Servant of God Elisabeth Leseur
DATES: 1866–1914 | **FEAST:** Not yet declared

Elisabeth and her husband lived a wealthy, sophisticated lifestyle in France. It was fashionable to think that religion was only necessary for the poor or ignorant. Elisabeth began to have a change of heart. She converted and became a Catholic. Her husband, even though he loved her, never accepted the fact that his wife believed in Catholicism. He ridiculed her and her faith. She accepted it all with patience and poured out her heart in her journals. She offered up her sufferings for him. After her death, Elisabeth's husband found her journals. Inspired by his wife's perseverance, he became a Catholic and later a Dominican priest.

St. Peter the Apostle
DATES: First Century | **FEAST:** June 29

When Peter met Jesus, he immediately left his nets to follow Him and become a "fisher of men." He was the first of the apostles to testify to Jesus as the Christ.

Peter persevered in following Christ despite some personal weaknesses, such as doubt, fear, and impulsiveness. Most famously he denied Jesus three times during the Passion, yet after the Resurrection he affirmed his love for Christ and the mandate to shepherd the Church as the first pope. His first letter encourages Christians to "set your hope fully upon the grace that is coming to you at the revelation of Jesus Christ" (1 Peter 1:13). Peter doggedly preached in the midst of persecution up to his own crucifixion for the faith.

St. María Venegas de la Torre
DATES: 1868–1959 | **FEAST:** July 30

María lived in Mexico when that country's government was trying to destroy Christianity within its borders. María was the head of a religious community, and she worked in hospitals with her religious sisters. During the persecutions of the 1920s, María kept her community safe and even opened two Catholic hospitals.

St. Monica
DATES: CA. 333–387 | **FEAST:** August 27

Augustine would possibly not have become a saint had it not been for his mother, Monica. For many years, Monica prayed for her wayward son from the time he was a young boy and even as he grew up and turned to pagan religions. Her unceasing prayers and tears were rewarded when her son converted to Christianity and became a great man of God.

Prayer

Dear Jesus,

You carried Your cross to Calvary even though You were tired, weak, and hurting. Please give me strength not to give up when life gets hard. Help me keep my eyes on You and Your kingdom, so I can do what is right even when I am tired and afraid.

MASTERING WITH TEMPERANCE

TEMPERANCE

Temperance can be represented by an olive wreath. In ancient times the olive wreath was the crown given to athletes and emperors. Temperance is often the fruit of hard work and gives the prize of authentic self-mastery. It crowns our decisions with a holy balance, joy, and inner peace.

"Every athlete exercises discipline in every way. They do it to win a perishable crown, but we an imperishable one."

—*1 Corinthians 9:25*

RELATED VIRTUES:

HONESTY   HUMILITY   MEEKNESS   MODERATION

MODESTY   ORDERLINESS   SELF-CONTROL

TEMPERANCE

KNOW IT

TEMPERANCE enables one to be moderate in the pleasure and use of created goods.

Temperance is cardinal virtue that brings order to our life, particularly our emotions and desires. It moderates the attractions of sense pleasure, providing balance in the use of the good things of this world. Temperance does not destroy our emotions or desires; rather it moderates them according to right reason. The temperate person is not bound by his instincts or desires, rather he can experience freedom, joy, and peace in the pursuit of goodness. The Christian who practices temperance is not attached to the things of the world, enabling him to be attached to the "one thing necessary" (Luke 10:42), Jesus Christ.

Cardinal Virtue of Temperance

CCC, 1809
CCC, 1837
CCC, 2517
CCC, 2518
CCC, 2519
CCC, 2733

Summa Theologiae

II–II.Q141–170, St. Thomas Aquinas

Echoing the Mystery

51-Cardinal Virtue of Temperance

Key Points

- Aims to perfect our emotions by moderating their attraction to pleasure
- Moderates desires and pleasure, particularly of food, drink, and sexuality
- Aims to create balance in the pursuit of pleasure

GUARD IT

The cardinal virtue of temperance aims to bring order into our desire and use of goods. At our Baptism, our heavenly Father gave us this virtue to aid us restoring this balance. The sins against temperance create havoc in our interior lives, leading us to be unreasonable and resistant to correction. Like all the virtues, temperance must be guarded from temptations.

Living temperance lies in the middle, in between the extremes of excess or defect. Sins of excess pursue pleasures by overindulgence beyond the order of right reason. Sins of defect are often motivated by fear. They repress or negate the natural desires to the detriment of the person. Temperance allows one to use properly and experience the goods and pleasure of this world.

GUARD IT

Sins Against Temperance

Intemperance is the pursuit of sensible pleasures outside the order of right reason. It "impairs" one's ability to recognize the good, the true, and the beautiful.

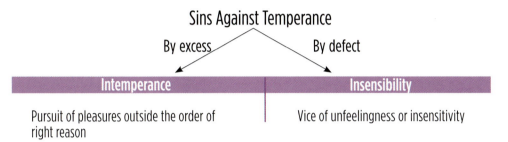

Related Virtue	Meaning	Opposing Vices
Abstinence	Moderation in the desire for food and touch	Gluttony
Sobriety	Moderation of the desire for drink and mind-altering substances	Drunkenness
Chastity	Successful integration of sexuality within the person and thus the inner unity of man in his bodily and spiritual being (CCC, 2337)	Lust
Purity	Mastery over the desires, thoughts, words, and actions that promote, foster, and initiate sexual union	Lack of sexual discipline
Virginity	Complete abstinence from sexual pleasure	
Meekness	Serenity of spirit while focusing on the needs of others	Anger
Clemency	A superior's moderation in punishing, or passing sentence upon, one who is subject to him	Desire for revenge
Modesty	Purity of heart in action, especially in regard to one's dress and speech	• Impurity, Lust • Boasting, Pride
	Modesty regulates our desire for attention. It also regulates our sense of fun (eutrapelia) as well as our desire or knowledge (studiousness). It preserves us from vain curiosity and immoderate use of games.	
Humility	Awareness that all one's gifts come from God; appreciation for the gifts of others; fruit of modesty	Pride

---

> *Slow down. Smell the flowers as you go by, and then you won't need too much of this world's goods. Enjoy your work and you won't need too much time off. Enjoy being at home and you won't have to go away so much.*
> —Fr. Benedict Groeschel, The Virtue Driven Life

> *Religions have a special role in this regard, for they teach people that authentic service requires sacrifice and self-discipline, which in turn must be cultivated through self-denial, temperance, and a moderate use of the world's goods.*
> —Pope Benedict XVI, Address, July 18, 2008

> *Do not rely on your strength in following the desires of your heart.*
> —Sirach 5:2

> *For the grace of God has appeared, saving all and training us to reject godless ways and worldly desires and to live temperately, justly, and devoutly in this age.*
> —Titus 2:11–12

> *But put on the Lord Jesus Christ, and make no provision for the desires of the flesh.*
> —Romans 13:14

TEMPERANCE

KNOW IT

GIFT OF FEAR OF THE LORD

RELATED BEATITUDE

The Gift of Fear of the Lord

"Blessed are the poor in spirit, for theirs is the kingdom of heaven."
—Matthew 5:3

The Gift of Fear of the Lord enables one to seek God Himself as one's only treasure. By living the beatitude "poor in spirit," one is freed from greed and pride.

Summa Theologiae

II–II.Q9, St. Thomas Aquinas

FEAR OF THE LORD brings forth the fear of offending God by sin.

By the cardinal virtue of temperance, we are given the grace to moderate our desires for pleasure. The **Gift of Fear of the Lord** in relation to the virtue of temperance enlightens us to the real danger of sin in the misuse of created goods and pleasures. It gives us a real horror of sin, not because we are afraid of punishment, but because it is a turning away from all that is good. It is "filial," the fear of a child who is confident in the love of his parents. Inspired by this, the Gift of Fear helps the disciple to shun those things that so easily tempt us away from God.

We normally use the word "fear" to describe an emotion. St. Thomas noted that there are four ways we speak of fear. The last, filial fear, is the context in which we speak about this gift of the Holy Spirit.

1. **Worldly Fear:** Love of the things of the world and fear of the loss of those goods
2. **Servile Fear:** Fear of the punishment as the principle motive for avoiding sin
3. **Initial Fear:** Moving toward filial fear, while still influenced by a fear of punishment
4. **Filial Fear:** The gift of the Holy Spirit that makes one revere God and avoid sin out of love for Him

Effects of the Gift of the Holy Spirit

- Sees God as a loving Father; puts His love at the center of one's life
- Regulates one's desires from within
- Horror and sorrow for sin because it is a loss of friendship with God
- Gives vigilance in avoiding sin and occasions of sin

GUARD IT

TEMPERANCE

The cardinal virtue of temperance and the Gift of Fear of the Lord are gifts given us at Baptism. Like any gift, they must be guarded from dangers.

- **Pride:** By hope, we trust in God. By pride, we trust in ourselves, leading us to disregard the commands of God that lead us toward salvation. It is an excessive self-esteem or self-love by which we desire attention, honor, or status beyond what is reasonable. It leads to unnecessary competition with others, and even with God Himself, closing one to God's love and the generosity of His plan for our salvation.

- **Presumption and Despair:** These two sins against hope stand in opposition to each other. Both fail to trust God for personal salvation. The first is when one presumes to take the burden of salvation upon one's self.

> *Now, therefore, Israel, what does the LORD, your God, ask of you but to fear the LORD, your God, to follow in all his ways, to love and serve the LORD, your God, with your whole heart and with your whole being.*
>
> —Deuteronomy 10:12

> *The fear of God consists wholly in love, and perfect love of God brings our fear of him to its perfection.*
> —St. Hilary, The Liturgy of the Hours

> *We must fear God out of love, not love Him out of fear.*
> —St. Francis de Sales

> *Much care is needed if this fear of God is to be thoroughly impressed upon the soul; though, if one has true love, it is quickly acquired.*
> —St. Teresa of Jesus

> *Those who fear the Lord seek to please him; those who love him are filled with his law.*
> —Sirach 2:16

> *Those who fear the Lord prepare their hearts and humble themselves before him.*
> —Sirach 2:17

> *His mercy is from age to age to those who fear him.*
> —Luke 1:50

TEMPERANCE

PRAY IT *LECTIO DIVINA*

Luke 16:19–31

"There was a rich man who dressed in purple garments and fine linen and dined sumptuously each day. And lying at his door was a poor man named Lazarus, covered with sores, who would gladly have eaten his fill of the scraps that fell from the rich man's table. Dogs even used to come and lick his sores. When the poor man died, he was carried away by angels to the bosom of Abraham. The rich man also died and was buried, and from the netherworld, where he was in torment, he raised his eyes and saw Abraham far off and Lazarus at his side. And he cried out, 'Father Abraham, have pity on me. Send Lazarus to dip the tip of his finger in water and cool my tongue, for I am suffering torment in these flames.' Abraham replied, 'My child, remember that you received what was good during your lifetime while Lazarus likewise received what was bad; but now he is comforted here, whereas you are tormented. Moreover, between us and you a great chasm is established to prevent anyone from crossing who might wish to go from our side to yours or from your side to ours.' He said, 'Then I beg you, father, send him to my father's house, for I have five brothers, so that he may warn them, lest they too come to this place of torment.' But Abraham replied, 'They have Moses and the prophets. Let them listen to them.' He said, 'Oh no, father Abraham, but if someone from the dead goes to them, they will repent.' Then Abraham said, 'If they will not listen to Moses and the prophets, neither will they be persuaded if someone should rise from the dead.'"

1. God's Word strikes the heart. What word or phrase touched your heart?

2. Describe the contrast between Lazarus and the rich man.

3. When the rich man died, what did he experience?

4. The dullness of sense arises from the sin of gluttony. In the parable it would seem that the rich man lost a sense of sin and sensitivity to those around him. Why didn't Abraham heed the rich man's request?

5. Ask this question in prayer: "Jesus, increase in me the gift of fear and show me how my sins offend You." Write down what He says to you.

PRAY IT

Pray an Act of Temperance

Heavenly Father,

You surround me with good things. I ask for the grace to use Your gifts rightly, allowing You to control my desires for the things You put into my life.

TEMPERANCE

LIVE IT — LOOKING TO THE SAINTS

VENERABLE MATT TALBOT

"Blessed are those who hunger and thirst for holiness."

Matt Talbot took ownership of his daily struggle with alcoholism. In fact, his honesty would make most of us uncomfortable. For forty-one years he did not drink and for those forty-one years all he wanted was a drink.

> **Mastering with Temperance**
>
> Sealed with the sign of the cross at his Baptism, Matt discovered his true identity as a son of God which empowered him to change.

Matt was born in 1856, the second of twelve children. His father was an alcoholic as well as most of his brothers. He started drinking on the job at the age of thirteen. For the next fifteen years all his thoughts, words, and actions were consumed with getting the next drink. To satisfy his consuming thirst, he stole, swindled, begged, and borrowed from anyone, including a blind beggar whose fiddle he stole.

Alone and without money or friends, Matt hit rock bottom. Plagued with loneliness, he went home. A mother's heart is unconquerable, and he was welcomed, but not without a bit of worry and concern.

Sealed with the sign of the cross at his Baptism, Matt discovered his true identity as a son of God which empowered him to change. Long before the Twelve Steps were formalized, Matt lived the basic principles. He started with a three month pledge not to drink. His daily meetings were frequent visits to the Church to attend Mass or to spend time in prayer pleading for inner strength. He took an inventory of his life and made amends by going regularly to Confession. The Franciscan Order became his community of support as his love for God and others marked his daily routine.

While he did not drink for forty-one years, his thirst for it never went away. He lived one day at a time tempering this insatiable thirst by living grafted onto the Vine—the One who gave us His Body and Blood to satisfy our hunger and thirst for holiness.

TEMPERANCE

LIVE IT

TEMPERANCE enables one to be moderate in the pleasure and use of created goods.

A Disciple of Christ living the virtue of temperance...

- ✓ Sees God as a loving Father
- ✓ Puts God's love at the center of one's life
- ✓ Regulates one's desires from within
- ✓ Experiences horror and sorrow for sin because it is a loss of friendship with God
- ✓ Gives vigilance in avoiding sin and occasions of sin
- ✓ Is meek (focusing on the needs of others)
- ✓ Is pure of heart in action, especially in regard to one's dress and speech
- ✓ Is humble (aware that all one's gifts come from God)

In the Words of St. Pope John Paul II...

A temperate man is one who is master of himself. One in whom passions do not prevail over reason, will, and even the "heart". A man who can control himself! If this is so, we can easily realize what a fundamental and radical value the virtue of temperance has. It is even indispensable, in order that man may be fully a man. It is enough to look at some one who, carried away by his passions, becomes a "victim" of them—renouncing of his own accord the use of reason (such as, for example, an alcoholic, a drug addict)—to see clearly that "to be a man" means respecting one's own dignity, and therefore, among other things, letting oneself be guided by the virtue of temperance. —St. Pope John Paul II, General Audience, Wednesday, 22 November 1978

Going Deeper in Temperance

FROM THE CATECHISM

Temperance moderates the attraction of the pleasures of the senses and provides balance in the use of created goods (*CCC*, 1838).

Temperance is the moral virtue that moderates the attraction of pleasures and provides balance in the use of created goods. It ensures the will's mastery over instincts and keeps desires within the limits of what is honorable. The temperate person directs the sensitive appetites toward what is good and maintains a healthy discretion: "Do not follow your inclination and strength, walking according to the desires of your heart" [Sirach 5:2; see 37:27–31]. Temperance is often praised in the Old Testament: "Do not follow your base desires, but restrain your appetites" [Sirach 18:30]. In the New Testament it is called "moderation" or "sobriety." We ought "to live sober, upright, and godly lives in this world" [Titus 2:12].

To live well is nothing other than to love God with all one's heart, with all one's soul and with all one's efforts; from this it comes about that love is kept whole and uncorrupted (through temperance). No misfortune can disturb it (and this is fortitude). It obeys only [God] (and this is justice), and is careful in discerning things, so as not to be surprised by deceit or trickery (and this is prudence). —*CCC*, 1809, quoting St. Augustine, *De moribus ecclesiae catholicae*, 1, 25, 46

The virtue of chastity comes under the cardinal virtue of temperance, which seeks to permeate the passions and appetites of the senses with reason (*CCC*, 2341).

Going Deeper in Fortitude

Purification of the Heart (*CCC*, 2517–2519)

The heart is the seat of moral personality: "Out of the heart come evil thoughts, murder, adultery, fornication..." [Matthew 15:19]. The struggle against carnal covetousness entails purifying the heart and practicing temperance:

> Remain simple and innocent, and you will be like little children who do not know the evil that destroys man's life (*CCC*, 2517, quoting The Shepherd of Hermas, Mandate 2, 1; see also *CCC*, 368, 1809).

The sixth beatitude proclaims, "Blessed are the pure in heart, for they shall see God" [Matthew 5:8]. "Pure in heart" refers to those who have attuned their intellects and wills to the demands of God's holiness, chiefly in three areas: charity [cf. 1 Timothy 4:3–9; 2 Timothy 2:22]; chastity or sexual rectitude [cf. Thessalonians 4:7; Colossians 3:5; Ephesians 4:19]; love of truth and orthodoxy of faith [cf. Titus 1:15; 1 Timothy 1:3–4; 2 Timothy 2:23–26]. There is a connection between purity of heart, of body, and of faith:

> The faithful must believe the articles of the Creed "so that by believing they may obey God, by obeying may live well, by living well may purify their hearts, and with pure hearts may understand what they believe." (*CCC*, 2518, quoting St. Augustine, *On Faith and the Creed*, 10, 25)

The "pure in heart" are promised that they will see God face to face and be like him (cf. 1 Corinthians 13:12; 1 John 3:2]. Purity of heart is the precondition of the vision of God. Even now it enables us to see according to God, to accept others as "neighbors"; it lets us perceive the human body—ours and our neighbor's—as a temple of the Holy Spirit, a manifestation of divine beauty (*CCC*, 2519).

The Blessed Virgin Mary and the Gifts of the Holy Spirit

The Annunciation to Mary and the Gift of Fear of the Lord

We pray and we hope that our prayers will be heard and answered. But what would we ever do if that answer took the form of a radiant angel speaking our name in the middle of our living room? It would probably terrify us just as it apparently terrified Mary. Gabriel soothes her with the words, "Do not fear, Mary" (Luke 1:30). The archangel frees Mary from her fright so as to bless her with the holy Fear of the Lord. For the Holy Spirit's Gift of Fear of the Lord disposes us to reverence God and to be completely devoted to him. Sanctified Fear of the Lord enables the Blessed Mother to show God the same devotion that he shows to her: "O highly favored daughter! The Lord is with you. Blessed are you among women" (Luke 1:28).

Fear of the Lord strengthens, renews, and refashions Mary's hope. In response to the angel's revelations, the Blessed Mother asks: "How can this be?" In the answer Gabriel gives, powerful hope is also given as well. Fear of the Lord helps Mary—and us—to see beyond whatever we consider constraining, unlikely, or impossible in our life. It opens up for us the boundlessness of God's mercy and providence. All the Lord asks of us to do in response is to rely utterly on his divine help. Fear of the Lord prevents us from ever disregarding God's assistance. Holy fear reminds us how crucial and urgent God's interaction in our life must remain in order for us to be happy, holy, and hope-filled.

At the same time, we see in Mary how "fear of the Lord is the beginning of wisdom" (Psalm 111:10). For in reverencing and believing the excellence of God revealed in the archangel Gabriel, the Blessed Mother manifests the right judgment she has about divine things. Her grace as Seat of Wisdom has begun to function in the reverent fear in which she receives God's messenger and accepts his message of Wisdom Incarnate.

Through this transforming experience of sanctified fear, Mary is called to look upon God in a new way. The angel announces that God is now her Spouse. St. Louis de Montfort writes: "The Holy Spirit became fruitful through Mary whom he espoused. To his faithful spouse, Mary, the Holy Spirit has communicated his ineffable gifts, and he has chosen her to dispense all that he possesses. The Holy Spirit says to Mary: 'You are still My Spouse, unswervingly faithful, pure and fruitful.'"

And what is Mary's response to all this? The profound humility that is Fear's effect. "Mary said, 'I am the servant of the Lord. Let it be done to me as you say'" (Luke 1:38). She gives herself to God as a servant...but not in a servile manner. Her concern is only to love God more, to fulfill his will, to avoid whatever might offend him, and to grow closer to him in love and devotion. In her utter poverty and humility, the Blessed Mother seeks nothing for herself. "Full of grace," Mary's Immaculate Heart is so absolutely disinclined to sin that Fear of the Lord prompts her to shun all evil as she awaits the birth of the Savior in perfect tranquility. And as we remain united to the Blessed Mother in her Fear of the Lord, her confidence and tranquility become our own. As Mary's life and song proclaim: "God's mercy is from age to age on those who fear him" (Luke 1:50).

"The Annunciation to Mary and the Gift of the Fear of the Lord," pg. 31. Cameron, Peter John O.P. *The Gifts of the Holy Spirit*. Veritas Series. Connecticut: Knights of Columbus, 2002.

MASTERING WITH TEMPERANCE

RELATED VIRTUE OF TEMPERANCE

HONESTY

MEANING

Sincerity, openness, and truthfulness in one's words and actions

OPPOSING TRAIT

Being dishonest in words and actions; telling lies

WAYS TO CULTIVATE

AGES 6 AND UP	Tell the truth even if it means you will get in trouble. "What I am saying is true."
AGES 10 AND UP	Not covering up mistakes, telling the truth in all situations; speaking up when someone is being treated wrongly.
AGES 12 AND UP	Be aware that God knows your heart; don't hide things from your parents or friends; seek to live and speak the truth even when it's hard.

Scripture

Proverbs 6:16–20	Mark 5:33	Colossians 3:9
Proverbs 10:9	Luke 19:8	2 Timothy 2:15
Proverbs 12:17–19	Acts 5:1–10	James 1:26
Proverbs 24:26	Ephesians 4:25	1 Peter 3:10–12
Daniel 13	Philippians 4:8–9	1 John 3:18
Matthew 21:28–31		

SAINTS

St. Stephen   DATES: First Century | FEAST: December 26

At the beginning of the Church, deacons were appointed to preach and to serve the Christians. One of these deacons was Stephen. When he preached to a crowd of Jewish people about the truth of Christ's death and resurrection, the leaders of the Jews had him arrested. They asked him about his preaching. He could have denied it, but he instead proclaimed the truth about Jesus Christ. St. Stephen's honesty led to his death, but also to his glorious place in heaven. He is the first martyr of the Church.

St. Bridget of Sweden   DATES: 1303–1373 | FEAST: July 23

God asked Bridget to deliver His truth to many people in positions of importance. As lady-in-waiting to the queen of Sweden, she helped the people of the court (including the king and queen) to live holier lives. She later went to Avignon and encouraged the pope to move back to Rome and serve as the Vicar of Christ. Bridget did not allow fear to keep her from speaking the truth to those who needed to hear it.

Bl. Henry Suso   DATES: ca. 1300–1366 | FEAST: March 2

Henry was a Dominican friar who frequently ended up in the wrong place at the wrong time. He was accused of theft, sacrilege, poisoning, and heresy at different points in his life; none of the accusations were true, as became evident by the end of his life. Henry lived an open and honest life, and so he was peaceful in spite of what others thought of him.

St. John Chrysostom   DATES: 347–407 | FEAST: September 13

John was the bishop of Constantinople, the capital city of the Byzantine Empire. He was such an excellent preacher that people began calling him "Chrysostom," which means "golden mouth." He used his eloquence to preach the truth. He spoke out against the rich who refused to help the poor, against priests who used bribes, and even against the empress. His honesty cost him; he was exiled from his home and never allowed to return.

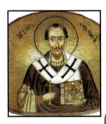

Prayer

Dear Jesus,

You said, "I am the Truth" (John 14:6). You have made me for Truth, because You have made me for Yourself! Help me be honest in all that I say and do, that I might know true happiness in You.

MASTERING WITH TEMPERANCE

RELATED VIRTUE OF TEMPERANCE

HUMILITY

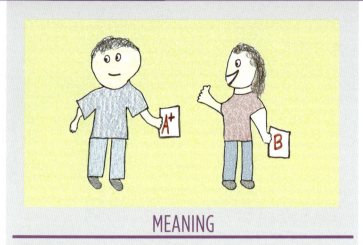

MEANING

Awareness that all one's gifts come from God and appreciation for the gifts of others

OPPOSING TRAIT

Failing to recognize the gifts of others; being too proud or having false humility

WAYS TO CULTIVATE

AGES 6 AND UP	Clap for someone who does a good job. "God gave me this talent."
AGES 10 AND UP	Give compliments to others and accept compliments from others; let others go in front of you in line.
AGES 12 AND UP	Show deference to others; acknowledge the accomplishments of others; look honestly at your strengths and weaknesses.

Scripture

Genesis 41:15–16	Matthew 11:29–30	Ephesians 4:2
1 Samuel 23:15–18	Luke 1:46–49	Philippians 2:3–11
Proverbs 15:33	Luke 9:47–48	1 Timothy 1:12–13
Sirach 43:13–33	Luke 14:10–11	1 Peter 3:3–4
Isaiah 6:5–8	Acts 3:11–16	James 4:6
Matthew 8:8		

SAINTS

St. Bernadette Soubirous   DATES: 1844–1879 | FEAST: April 16

When Bernadette was a young girl living in Lourdes, France, she saw a vision of Our Lady. "I am the Immaculate Conception," Mary said to her. Although Bernadette did not know what that meant, she did all that Our Lady asked her to do. A chapel was built, and Lourdes is now a place of pilgrimage and healing for the sick. Bernadette became a nun and did not tell people about the visions. She showed great humility by never seeking fame or recognition, even though Our Lady had chosen her to be God's messenger.

St. Bonaventure   DATES: 1221–1274 | FEAST: July 15

Bonaventure lived at the same time as the great St. Thomas Aquinas, and he was equally renowned for his knowledge. He and Aquinas were both asked to write prayers for the celebration of the new feast of Corpus Christi. When Bonaventure saw the office that Aquinas had written, he did not even finish his. In his humility he saw that what Aquinas had written was much more worthy to be prayed by the Church.

St. Joseph of Cupertino   DATES: 1603–1663 | FEAST: September 18

Joseph was known to other children as "the gaper" because he left his mouth open most of the time. He was not a good student. When he entered the Capuchin order, he helped in the kitchen and the stables. He struggled with his seminary classes, but he had a deep love for Jesus. Eventually Joseph was allowed to become a priest. He was then nicknamed "the flying friar" because of his God-given ability to levitate. In the face of both teasing and fame, Joseph remained humble and cheerful.

St. Gemma Galgani   DATES: 1878–1903 | FEAST: April 11

Even as a child Gemma would say, "Gemma can do nothing, but Gemma and Jesus can do all things." Throughout her life she retained this simplicity. Jesus granted her many visions of Him, but she never thought she was special.

Gemma suffered a great deal, and she offered it all for the salvation of souls. After her mother and father died, she spent most of her time taking care of her younger siblings.

Prayer

Dear Jesus,

You said, "Learn from Me, for I am meek and humble of heart" (Matthew 11:29). You are God, yet You became little out of love for me. I desire to become little for love of You. Help me to be honest about my strengths and weaknesses. May You be glorified in everything that I do!

MASTERING WITH TEMPERANCE

RELATED VIRTUE OF TEMPERANCE

MEEKNESS

MEANING

Serenity of spirit while focusing on the needs of others

OPPOSING TRAIT

Giving in to anger and losing one's temper when working or playing with others

WAYS TO CULTIVATE

AGES 6 AND UP — When you get upset, count to ten before you react. "I will wait until you are finished."

AGES 10 AND UP — Walk away when you are angry instead of fighting.

AGES 12 AND UP — Remain calm; allow others to go first; wait without expecting people to notice your patience.

Scripture

Genesis 45:3–5
Psalm 45:4
Proverbs 16:19
Proverbs 20:3
Isaiah 66:2
Zephaniah 3:11–12
Matthew 5:5
Matthew 5:28–44
John 18:22–23
Ephesians 4:26–27
Colossians 3:12–13
Hebrews 12:14–15
1 Peter 5:5

SAINTS

Bl. Anthony Grassi
DATES: 1592–1671 | **FEAST:** December 13

Anthony was a brilliant young priest of the Oratorian Fathers. He was a kind and serene man. He loved the rule of his order, and his meekness kept him from being severe when teaching other Oratorians to follow it. He was often able to bring peace to troubled situations. On his deathbed he reconciled two Oratorian brothers who were having an angry dispute.

Ven. Pierre Toussaint
DATES: 1766–1853 | **FEAST:** Not Yet Declared

Pierre's family was from Haiti, but he was a slave to an American family who settled in New York. When the father of the family died suddenly, Pierre could have obtained his freedom. The man's widow was in difficulty, and Pierre stayed and worked as a hairdresser for the fashionable ladies of New York City to support her. Everywhere he went people were drawn to him because of his gentleness and kindness. They gave him money to help others. He helped pay for Old St. Patrick's Church on Mulberry Street in New York City and he cared for many sick people.

St. John de Britto
DATES: 1647–1693 | **FEAST:** February 14

John was a native of Lisbon, Portugal, who became a missionary in India. The great men of India had no interest in converting from Hinduism. John learned their customs and traditions, even dressing the way they did. He slowly won their trust by his respect for them. They were willing to listen to him talk about Jesus, and some of them converted.

St. Thérèse of the Child Jesus
DATES: 1873–1897 | **FEAST:** October 1

Thérèse was a young French girl who entered a Carmelite convent when she was fifteen years old. She practiced the virtue of meekness by loving all the other nuns, even those who caused her annoyance. She strove to show her love not by great or heroic things but by little actions for God and her sisters. Her sisters in religion, upon her death, hardly knew of her spiritual greatness.

Today St. Thérèse is a co-patroness of the missions and a Doctor of the Church. Her autobiography and other writings have brought many to a deeper walk with God.

Prayer

Dear Jesus,

Be king of my heart, especially when I am frustrated or angry. In those moments give me the grace to use all my emotions for the good.

TEMPERANCE

MASTERING WITH TEMPERANCE

RELATED VIRTUE OF TEMPERANCE

MODERATION

MEANING

Attention to balance in one's life

OPPOSING TRAIT

Giving in to being excessive in one or more areas of one's life

WAYS TO CULTIVATE

AGES 6 AND UP — Resist the desire to play during work time in class or at home.
"No thank you, I have had enough."

AGES 10 AND UP — Limit how much food you eat; limit time spent on the computer.

AGES 12 AND UP — Set limits for yourself; create a balance with homework and leisure activity; fast from food you enjoy.

Scripture

Psalm 119:97	Sirach 32:11–13	Galatians 5:13
Proverbs 17:27	Matthew 14:23	Galatians 6:4–5
Proverbs 23:4	Matthew 23:23–26	Colossians 4:6
Proverbs 25:27	Luke 11:37	1 Timothy 3:2–3
Ecclesiastes 3:1	1 Corinthians 6:12	1 Timothy 6:17

SAINTS

St. John XXIII   DATES: 1881–1963 | FEAST: October 11

Growing up in Italy, Angelo began keeping a prayer journal when he was a teenager. He became a priest and later worked for the Vatican as the pope's ambassador to other countries. He was given very difficult assignments during World War II. The cardinals elected him Pope in 1958. He kept his prayer journal his whole life. He balanced his many responsibilities with time for rest and prayer. He even had time to take a walk every day. He never let himself worry too much either. When he said his night prayers, he would tell God, "Well, I did my best. It's Your Church, so I'm going to bed now."

St. John of God   DATES: 1495–1555 | FEAST: March 8

John was a Spaniard who, until he was forty, lived a selfish and wicked life. Through God's grace he had sudden conversion, and he began to perform such strange penances that he was put in a hospital for the insane. St. John of Avila advised him to moderate his penance by performing simple acts of charity. His moderation helped him grow in sanctity, and many people asked his help in growing closer to God.

Bl. John Henry Newman   DATES: 1801–1890 | FEAST: October 9

John Henry was an Anglican priest who decided to study the history of Christianity. This led him to the realization that the Catholic Church is the true Church, and he converted. He became a Catholic priest and lived a simple life in one of St. Philip Neri's oratories.

As a priest, John Henry balanced prayer, friendships, and study. He spent much of his time writing books to explain the beauty of the Catholic understanding of the world.

St. Francis de Sales   DATES: 1567–1622 | FEAST: January 24

Francis was known as "the gentle bishop," which is why the pope sent him to Geneva where there were many disputes between Catholics and Protestants. The pope needed someone who could bring some balance and peace to the situation. Francis, however, wasn't always so gentle. As a young man he worked hard to master his temper and moderate his desires. This internal struggle opened him up to allow God's grace to work through him. Many people came to him because of his wise advice. His spiritual writings continue to guide Christians in the ways of holiness.

Prayer

Dear Jesus,

Help me to keep a balance in my life, using created things properly and in the right amount that is best for me. I need Your help to set limits for myself in doing things that I enjoy, such as using video games, playing outside, eating, and using my phone and the internet. Lead me on Your way of happiness!

MASTERING WITH TEMPERANCE

RELATED VIRTUE OF TEMPERANCE

MODESTY

MEANING

Purity of heart in action, especially in regards to dress and speech

OPPOSING TRAIT

Choosing to dress or act in a way inconsistent with one's dignity as a child of God

WAYS TO CULTIVATE

AGES 6 AND UP	Try not to show off. "I would like to dress in private."
AGES 10 AND UP	Follow the dress code; dress and act with dignity as a child of God.
AGES 12 AND UP	Recognize your dignity as a person; ask yourself if you are advertising or calling attention to yourself; dress modestly.

Scripture

Genesis 3:21	Romans 12:3	Galatians 6:14
Psalm 115:1	1 Corinthians 3:5–7	Philippians 2:5
Proverbs 25:6–7	1 Corinthians 6:19–20	Colossians 4:6
Proverbs 27:1–2	2 Corinthians 10:17	1 Timothy 2:9
Matthew 20:25–28	2 Corinthians 12:5–6	1 Peter 5:5

SAINTS

St. Maria Goretti DATES: 1890–1902 | FEAST: July 6

Maria Goretti was a peasant girl who lived in Italy. Her father died, and her mother had to work hard on the farm to make a living for the family. Maria spent her days keeping house and caring for her younger siblings.

When a neighbor boy tried to force Maria to act against purity and modesty, she refused and fought against him. She remained firm in her modesty, even though the boy threatened her life. He fatally stabbed her, and she forgave him before she died.

St. Thomas Aquinas DATES: ca. 1225–1275 | FEAST: January 28

Thomas' wealthy family wanted him to become a powerful abbot, but Thomas wanted only to be a humble Dominican friar. He had a brilliant mind, but he was so wary of showing off that some of his fellow students thought he was unintelligent.

Thomas became the Church's greatest theologian. Still, at the end of his life, he said that everything he had written was "only straw" compared to God's greatness.

St. André Bessette DATES: 1845–1937 | FEAST: January 6

André Bessette was known as the miracle worker at St. Joseph's Oratory in Canada. Many people with illnesses or injuries came to this doorkeeper of his community for help. He prayed for them to St. Joseph, and many were healed.

Although God's grace was evidently working through him, Brother André never took credit for the healings. He insisted that they were all due to St. Joseph's intercession.

St. Bruno DATES: 1030–1101 | FEAST: October 6

Bruno was encouraged by his bishop to begin a monastery, and so he founded the Carthusian order. Carthusians spend nearly all of their days in silent prayer and work. Bruno's brothers copied the Bible by hand. Hearing of Bruno's skill at organization, Pope Urban II wanted to honor him with a position in the Vatican. Bruno respectfully declined and remained with his Carthusian brothers until his death.

Prayer

Dear Jesus,
Give me a pure heart like that of Your holy Mother! Through baptism I have the gift of the Spirit living inside of me. Please increase in me the gift of the fear of the Lord, so that I may never sadden You by the way I dress, act, or speak.

MASTERING WITH TEMPERANCE

RELATED VIRTUE OF TEMPERANCE

ORDERLINESS

MEANING

Keeping oneself physically clean and neat and one's belongings in good order

OPPOSING TRAIT

Disorder with regard to one's space and physical appearance

WAYS TO CULTIVATE

AGES 6 AND UP	Put things back after using them. "I will come after I put my toys away."
AGES 10 AND UP	Use a planner to keep track of your homework; clean up before your parents ask.
AGES 12 AND UP	Pick up after yourself; leave things in order; take pride in your appearance; use a planner to keep track of your responsibilities and appointments.

Scripture

Genesis 1:1–27	Matthew 6:16–18	Romans 12:2
Exodus 40:16–33	Luke 15:8–9	1 Corinthians 14:40
Judith 10:1–3	Luke 16:10	Ephesians 6:14–17
Psalm 8	John 9:6–7	1 Timothy 3:4–5
Psalm 104	John 20:6–7	2 Timothy 2:15
Proverbs 9:1–2		

SAINTS

St. Benedict — DATES: 480–547 | FEAST: July 11

When Benedict became a monk, he went to a cave at Subiaco. At that time monasteries were not very organized, and sometimes this was problematic when difficulties arose. Other monks noticed Benedict's holiness and humility, so they asked him to be their leader. He wrote a rule for a way of life. He wanted his monks to live balanced lives and grow in virtue. The rule helped them worship God throughout the day in their prayer, work, and recreation.

Bl. Humbert of Romans — DATES: ca. 1200–1277 | FEAST: July 14

Humbert, was elected to lead the Dominican order when many men and women had joined and the order was in need of better organization. Humbert, who had been a lawyer, established the liturgy, the houses, the missions, and the constitutions (or rules) in a clear and understandable way. His work gave the Dominicans the freedom to carry on the work of God in their teaching and preaching.

St. Raymond of Peñafort — DATES: ca. 1175–1275 | FEAST: January 7

Raymond was a Dominican priest who helped train seminarians to be priests. Pope Gregory IX asked him to help with a large project. None of the Church's laws was organized. During his spare time, Raymond collected and organized all the decrees of the Church. His book was used as the main reference for the next eight hundred years.

St. Albert the Great — DATES: 1206–1280 | FEAST: November 15

Albert was a Dominican friar who is best known as a brilliant scientist. While many scientists of his time were searching for magical formulas for making gold, Albert realized that God had created order in the universe and that it could be studied scientifically. He became an authority in biology, astronomy, physics, geology, and many other areas of science. He taught others to see the beauty of God's order in creation.

Prayer

Oh Infinite Beauty,

In Your wisdom, You created all things with perfect order. Orderliness brings peace, beauty, harmony, and joy! Please help me to keep order in my own life so that I may respect those things You have entrusted to me. In particular, please assist me in keeping my appearance, room/locker, and workspace clean and neat.

MASTERING WITH TEMPERANCE

RELATED VIRTUE OF TEMPERANCE

SELF-CONTROL

MEANING

Joyful mastery over one's passions and desires

OPPOSING TRAIT

Being excessive in words or actions, acting impulsively

WAYS TO CULTIVATE

AGES 6 AND UP — Listen to others while they speak; do not interrupt. "I will raise my hand before I speak."

AGES 10 AND UP — Control your reactions when you feel angry or frustrated.

AGES 12 AND UP — Fast; restrain yourself from saying or doing everything you desire; practice restraint in words and actions.

Scripture

Proverbs 16:32	1 Corinthians 10:13	Titus 1:8
Proverbs 25:28	Galatians 5:22–23	James 1:19–21
Sirach 11:8	Ephesians 4:29–32	James 3:5–10
Romans 12:1–2	Philippians 4:8–9	1 Peter 5:6–8
1 Corinthians 9:24–27	2 Timothy 1:6–7	

SAINTS

St. Perpetua
DATES: ca. 181–203 | **FEAST:** March 7

In the early days of the Church, Perpetua was a young, wealthy woman who was imprisoned for her refusal to worship anyone but Christ. She and her fellow prisoners were to be killed by being thrown to wild animals. All the prospective martyrs were terrified, but Perpetua set aside her fears, encouraged the others, and went bravely to her death for love of Christ.

St. Anthony of Egypt
DATES: ca. 251–356 | **FEAST:** January 17

Anthony of Egypt went to Mass one day and heard the Gospel; "Go, sell all you have, and give to the poor. Then come, follow me" (Matthew 18:22). Immediately he decided to obey the Gospel. After selling all his goods, he went to the desert to live in silence and prayer.

Anthony worked hard to master his passions: he fasted, he had a regular schedule, and he prayed constantly. Eventually he taught other monks to focus only on God.

Bl. Charles de Foucauld
DATES: 1858–1916 | **FEAST:** December 1

As a child, Charles was rather wild and got into his share of trouble. When he was an officer in the French army, he had a profound conversion. He began to practice self-control and make sacrifices to help him focus on God. He became a priest and was given permission to live a life of prayer in the Sahara desert. In 1916 there was an outbreak of violence in the area. In December Charles was killed in the cross fire of two political rivals.

St. Kateri Tekakwitha
DATES: 1656–1680 | **FEAST:** July 14

Kateri Tekakwitha was a Mohawk Indian who became a Christian when Jesuit missionaries visited her tribe's village in what is now New York. She loved the Christians so much that she went back with them to their mission in Canada. There she lived simply and worked hard to provide for herself and those with whom she lived. She lived a simple life so she could share what she had with others.

Prayer

Dear Jesus,

Thank You for all the desires You have given me, because they remind me of the desire in my heart that only You can fill! Help me to control my tongue when I am supposed to be silent; my hands when I am supposed to keep them to myself; my eyes when I am supposed to be focused on a particular person or thing; and my ears to listen to only those things I am supposed to hear.

Section 3 | Who Lives and Teaches Virtue?

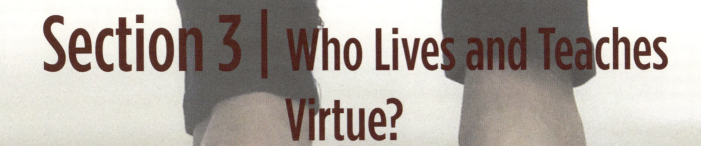

One truth that is evident in the Gospels is that following Jesus leads to happiness and interior freedom.

Living Virtuously

What was from the beginning,
what we have heard,
what we have seen with our eyes,
what we looked upon
and touched with our hands
concerns the Word of life—
for the life was made visible;
we have seen it and testify to it
and proclaim to you the eternal life
that was with the Father and was made visible to us—
what we have seen and heard
we proclaim now to you,
so that you too may have fellowship with us;
for our fellowship is with the Father
and with his Son, Jesus Christ.
We are writing this so that our joy may be complete.
1 John 1:1–4

Heard, Seen, Touched

St. John, the apostle and evangelist, gives testimony to what he experienced personally. In hearing, seeing, and touching Jesus of Nazareth, John has come to know and believe that he was hearing, seeing, and touching the eternal Son of God. To those hearing his message, he is credible, giving testimony primarily by the witness of his life.

This passage gives a sort of blueprint of discipleship. A disciple is one who is invited by Christ to share in His own life. Once accepted, the disciple is brought into *koinonía* with Him. This Greek word denotes fellowship, relationship, communion. This communion is transformative, giving the disciple a new orientation and purpose. It influences every decision and every action. Once brought into fellowship with Christ, the disciple can only respond by proclaiming his experience of Christ. This call to discipleship continues through the centuries. It is the same Jesus who calls us now to experience the same joy and fellowship with Him. He "is the same yesterday, today, and forever" (Hebrews 13:8). The question becomes: **How are you being called to live as His disciple?**

Living Virtuously

One truth that is evident in the Gospels is that following Jesus leads to happiness and interior freedom. His call is transformative, because individuals immediately and radically follow Him. We see this manifested in the Gospels as Christ invited individuals to follow Him. John experienced this when he left his father and his fishing nets at the call of Jesus. The apostle Matthew was a tax collector, sitting at his customs post. Christ looked upon him with the eyes of mercy and called him. "'Follow Me.' And he got up and followed Him" (Mark 2:14). The brevity of the Gospel account reveals to us Matthew's readiness. Once despised—both for his profession, with its proclivity to greed, and for his association with a government foreign to the People of God—Matthew becomes a model of discipleship, testifying to the marvelous effects of God's grace in one's life.

Zacchaeus also was a tax collector, trying to see Jesus as the crowds pressed around Him. In his desire to see Jesus, he ran ahead to climb a sycamore tree. Christ saw him and said, "Zacchaeus, come down quickly, for today I must stay at your house" (Luke 19:1–10). Notice the rapid succession of events, and how liberating it was for Zacchaeus. He "came down quickly," "received him with joy," gave away half of his possessions to poor, and repaid "four times over" to anyone he had extorted. What true magnificence! In a single encounter, Zacchaeus was set free and transformed.

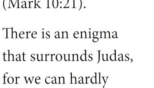

Following Jesus leads to happiness and interior freedom.

Each of these encounters, and others recounted in the Gospel, led to a wholeness, a reintegration of the person. To understand this point even more it is helpful to look at one who did not accept Christ's invitation to discipleship. The rich young man lived a good life, he followed the commandments. He was a good person. "Jesus, looking at him, loved him" and invited him to leave everything to follow Him. He was being invited into intimate fellowship with Jesus. With a tragic brevity, Mark tells us that "his face fell, and he went away sad, for he had many possessions" (Mark 10:21).

There is an enigma that surrounds Judas, for we can hardly comprehend how someone who lived so intimately with Christ could betray Him in that way. A careful reading of the Gospels reveals his gradual turning away from the face of God. He allowed some other voice to resound in his ears, he looked upon money as his treasure, something else touched his heart. When the woman anointed the feet of Jesus, and the aroma of the perfume filled the house, he could not rejoice in the shared communion among the followers of Christ. Instead he spoke out in contempt, hardening his heart (Matthew 26:6–13).

But Christ promises "abundant life" to those who accept His invitation (John 10:10). He says that "the kingdom of heaven is at hand" (Matthew 3:2, Mark 1:15). It is here, now. It began the moment of our Baptism and begins again every time we renew our baptismal commitment. St. Catherine of Siena once commented on this saying that "every step of the way to heaven is heaven."

Living Virtuously

Does this mean our lives will be free from suffering or sorrow? Well, no, for the simple reason that Christ's life was not void from suffering and sorrow. But His life gives meaning to it. When we draw near to Christ, appropriating and assimilating to ourselves the whole reality of Christ's Incarnation and Redemption, then we can find ourselves. With the certainty of faith, the disciple can look upon the cross and know that it was there, on the cross, that Christ restored us to our dignity as sons and daughters of God. Death loses it sting. Because, instead of being the "wages of sin," Christ has now made it means of my redemption (cf. Romans 6:23). Suffering and sorrow can now be embraced. In fact, Christ made it a condition of discipleship. "If anyone wishes to come after me, he must deny himself and take up his cross daily and follow me" (Luke 9:23).

A Disciple of Christ Hears Him

The Latin *obedire* (to obey) has at its root *audire* (to listen, to hear). The sin of Adam and Eve was a sin of disobedience. Instead of listening to the voice of their heavenly Father, they listened to the voice of the tempter. Mary's obedience untied the knot of the original disobedience. She set into motion the paradigm of holiness, giving us a model of holiness to imitate.

To hear Christ requires interior and exterior silence. We hear His voice through the Scriptures, through the Church, through the sacraments, through a life of prayer. The theological virtue of faith opens our ears to hear God's voice, to believe in Him and assent to all that He has revealed. It then opens our eyes to see the world differently.

Throughout the Old Testament, there are two converging, yet opposite, themes. On one hand there is Israel's desire to see God. "'Come,' says my heart, 'seek his face;' your face, Lord, do I seek" (Psalm 27:8)! On the other hand, there is Israel's inability to be in the presence of God. When Moses begs the Lord to let him see His glory, God, in His mercy, sets Moses in the cleft of the rock, covers him with His hand, and allows Moses to see His back as He passes by (Exodus 33:18–23). This anthropomorphic way of speaking of God is meant to reveal to us His august holiness. As sinners, we just cannot withstand it. "Blessed are the clean of heart, for they will see God" (Matthew 5:8). Sin has deep roots in us. By His Incarnation, Christ took on a human face so that we can see God. By His Passion and Death, he bore our sins in His body upon the cross, so that, free from sin, we might live for righteousness. "By His wounds you have been healed" (1 Peter 2:24).

Just as a vine needs pruning, so do our hearts. Daily we are called to uproot sin. This requires a daily commitment to free our hearts from distractions, sin, and vice. The virtues aid in cultivating this life of freedom. An integrated life leads to the purity of heart that enables one to see God. A life of prayer keeps our eyes fixed on Christ. When we look upon Him, He looks at us and comes to dwell within us. The theological virtue of hope anchors us in Christ. Christ in His full humanity has gone before us into heaven as our "forerunner," desiring us to follow after Him (cf. Hebrews 6:19–20).

> Just as a vine needs pruning, so do our hearts.

Living Virtuously

A Disciple of Christ Touches Him

Adam and Eve walked with God in the Garden, they lived in easy fellowship with their heavenly Father. More amazing still is the communion we have with God in the sacraments. "We run straight into His arms. And when we let Him get close to us, He teaches us, feeds us, transforms us, heals us, and becomes one with us in the Holy Sacrifice of the Mass" (*Youcat*, 168). Each time we receive Holy Communion, we take into our very bodies the Body of Christ. We touch Him in the sacraments. The fellowship of the Garden is nothing compared to the communion we have in Christ.

The Mass ends with a command, "Go, in the peace of Christ." A dynamic Eucharistic vision is able to see Christ in our brothers and sisters. We are created in the image and likeness of the Triune God—Father, Son, and Holy Spirit. We are called to live in fellowship with each other in relationships of charity and truth. This is opposite of this is a radical autonomy that becomes closed off in self-centeredness and isolation. John Paul Sartre said, "Hell is other people," but he could not have been further from the truth. Hell is utter isolation, cut off from the very Source of goodness and thus unable to be relationship with others.

The theological virtue of charity enables us to have a Eucharistic vision, seeing Christ in the least. In the parable of the sheep and the goats, Jesus identifies Himself with "one of the least brethren of Mine:" the hungry, the thirsty, the stranger, the naked, the ill, and the imprisoned (cf. Matthew 25:31–46). When we touch our brothers and sisters in need, we touch Christ. When we give ourselves, we discover ourselves. We are able to live fully by living a life marked by the corporal and spiritual works of mercy, seeking to extend God's love to those who do not yet know Him. We become the "good tree" that bears fruit.

A Disciple of Christ Testifies and Proclaims Him

When John and Andrew first met Christ, they spent the day with Him. They encountered Christ and allowed Him to transform their lives. They could hardly contain it. Andrew immediately went to his brother with the bold proclamation, "We have found the Messiah." Then Philip did the same and found Nathaniel (cf. John 1:41, 45). We are called to do the same. A Christian is not saved in isolation. St. Paul grappled with this reality when he cried out: "But how can they call on him in whom they have not believed? And how can they believe in him of whom they have not heard? And how can they hear without someone to preach? And how can people preach unless they are sent? As it is written, 'How beautiful are the feet of those who bring good news!'" (Romans 10:14–15) By the sacrament of Confirmation, each one of us was "sent," commissioned to share the Good News. We are reminded of this task at the end of each Mass. Catholic education fits within this missionary task of the Church. We are called to give testimony to Christ whom we have heard, seen, and touched. When our testimony comes out of that lived relationship with Christ, only then we are credible witnesses. As others are brought into fellowship with Christ, we will be able to say with John that **"our joy is complete."**

Living as a Disciple of Christ

 *Remaining in Him*

To live as a disciple of Christ requires a personal commitment to cultivating your interior life. Just as sap brings life to the branches of a tree, the more you remain in Christ as a branch grafted on the vine, the more freely the Holy Spirit will be with you in your daily life. This is the path to interior freedom and happiness. St. Catherine of Siena described the relationship this way: "The soul is in God and God in the soul, just as the fish is in the sea and the sea is in the fish."

To become a credible witness:

1. Seek Conversion

As a disciple of Christ, you are called to daily conversion; that is, striving each day to live in truth and freedom. A daily examination enables you to experience God's mercy and start each day anew in Christ.

- PRESENCE: Place yourself in God's presence
- PRAISE AND GRATITUDE: Recall the blessings of the day (joys/sorrows)
- PROCESS: Reflect upon the events of the day (your thoughts and feelings)
- PENANCE AND CONVERSION: Acknowledge your sins and resolve to change
- PLAN and PROMISE: Intentionally plan for a new day receptive to God's grace

(Use the Happiness Is *pamphlet, a virtue-based examen, to identify the virtues you need to cultivate along your path of conversion. See p. 155.)*

2. Commit to Pray

Learn to listen to God through prayer and reading His Word. Ask God how He may use you to be a witness to others.

(Use the "Pray It" sections for each virtue as a guide for lectio divina. See p. 28–29, 40–41, 53, 63, 77, 101, 116–117.)

3. Live Virtuously

Live the virtues in your every day life. Intentionally cultivate the life of virtue to overcome habits of sin in your life.

(Review Virtue Chart p. 138–139 and Seven Capital Sins Chart p. 137.)

4. Give of Self

Serve others by incorporating the corporal and spiritual works of mercy into your life.

(Review the Corporal and Spiritual Works of Mercy on p. 156.)

TRANSFORMATION IN CHRIST | SEVEN CAPITAL SINS

PRIDE	Undue self-esteem or self-love, which seeks attention and honor and sets oneself in competition with God	—*Virtues to Cultivate*—	*James 4:6*
—Manifestations—	Vanity	Arrogance	Boasting	Haughtiness	Ambition	Ostentation	Love of limelight	Hypocrisy	Vainglory	HUMILITY	HONESTY	
	Disobedience	OBEDIENCE	
	Despising others	Holding others in contempt	Discord	Obstinate (hardheadedness)	Quarreling	CHARITY	KINDNESS	

ENVY	Resentment or sadness at another's good fortune, and the desire to have it for oneself	—*Virtues to Cultivate*—	*Mark 7:21–23*
—Manifestations—	Nasty and unkind remarks about others	KINDNESS	
	Constantly belittling others	Gossip	Detraction	Backbiting	Calumny	SINCERITY	
	False judgments	Discord	Hatred	Spirit of enmity	CHARITY	
	Jealousy – inordinate love of self and fear of losing something	HUMILITY	

ANGER	An emotion which is not in itself wrong but which, when it is not controlled by reason or hardens into resentment and hate becomes one of the seven sins	—*Virtues to Cultivate*—	*Ephesians 4: 26–27*
—Manifestations—	Undue sensitiveness	Impatience	Irritability	Grumbling	Fault-finding	MEEKNESS	PATIENCE	RESPECT	
	Quarreling	Discord	Contention	Argumentativeness	HUMILITY	HONESTY	CHARITY	
	Gossip	Detraction	Defamation	Calumny	JUSTICE	
	Excessive anger	Revengeful	Retaliation	Fiery	Reactive anger	Repressed anger	Temper tantrums	Cruel	Violent	SELF-CONTROL	

ACEDIA (SLOTH)	A form of sadness when encountering God and God's ways (spiritual sloth) caused by neglecting the faith and moral life	—*Virtues to Cultivate*—	*Matthew 25:26, 28–30*
—Manifestations—	Uneasy restlessness of the mind	Excessive curiosity	Talkativeness	Instability of place and purpose	TEMPERANCE	SELF-CONTROL	CHASTITY	MODERATION	
	Apathy	Listlessness	Torpor with regard to one's need for salvation	PERSEVERANCE	INDUSTRIOUSNESS	MAGNIFICENCE	
	Faintheartedness	"Small soul"	Lacking courage to pursue spiritual life	FORTITUDE	MAGNANIMITY	
	Despair	HOPE	
	Nursing grudges	Spitefulness	Maliciousness	MODERATION	

AVARICE (GREED)	Inordinate desire for earthly things	—*Virtues to Cultivate*—	*1 Timothy 6:10*
—Manifestations—	Deceit	Perjury	Lying	Cheating	Craftiness	Shrewdness	HONESTY	
	Treachery	Fraud	Betrayal	JUSTICE	LOYALTY	
	Restlessness	Hardness of heart	Violence	GENEROSITY	

GLUTTONY	Overindulgence in food or drinks	—*Virtues to Cultivate*—	*Luke 16:19–31*
—Manifestations—	Dullness of sense	Talkativeness	Vulgarity	Impurity	TEMPERANCE	
	Intemperance	Overindulgence in food and drink	MODERATION	
	Ruin of health	PRUDENCE	

LUST	Inordinate desire for sexual pleasure or inordinate enjoyment of sexual pleasure	—*Virtues to Cultivate*—	*Matthew 5:28*
—Manifestations—	Internal acts: Intentionally dwelling on fantasies	Impure thoughts and desires (Sins forbidden by ninth commandment)	TEMPERANCE	SELF-CONTROL	CHASTITY	MODERATION	MODESTY	
	External acts: Sins against chastity	Impurity	Viewing pornography	Adultery	Fornication (Sins forbidden by the sixth commandment)	PURITY	LOYALTY	
	Blindness of mind: Prevents one from thinking clearly	Inconsideration	Thoughtlessness	Inordinate self-love	**TO PRESERVE A PURE HEART:** *Life of Chastity, Life of Charity, Life of Committed Truth*	
	Weakening of the will	Inconstancy	Hastiness	Imprudence	PRUDENCE	FORTITUDE	
	Disordered attachment to the world	Despair	Hatred of God	FAITH	HOPE	

Disciple of Christ Virtues

IN BAPTISM WE ARE GRAFTED ONTO CHRIST THE VINE He enters us and remains in us as long as we desire His presence. By freely choosing to live as one with Christ, we permit Him to transform us from within. This life in Christ is rooted in the virtues and gifts received at Baptism (*CCC*, 1266).

"If faith is like the root, charity is like the sap that nourishes the trunk and rises into the branches, the network of virtues, to produce the delicious fruit of good works" (Servais Pinckaers, O.P., *Morality: The Catholic View*, South Bend, St. Augustine Press, 2001).

Disciple of Christ Virtues guide educators, parents, and students in identifying virtues which need to be cultivated. Each corresponding "Opposing Trait" highlights a pattern of behavior which needs change in order for one to mature in virtue.

Human virtues acquired by education, by deliberate acts, and by perseverance ever-renewed in repeated efforts are purified and elevated by divine grace. With God's help, they forge character and give facility in the practice of the good. The virtuous man is happy to practice them. (CCC, 1810)

"GOD GIVES THE GROWTH" (1 CORINTHIANS 3:7).

VIRTUE	MEANING	OPPOSING TRAIT	WAYS TO CULTIVATE
JUSTICE (Fairness)	Enables one to give to each, beginning with God, what is due him	Failing to see what is owed to each by virtue of his dignity	Recognize what is due to God first and then to others.
Affability	Being easy to approach and talk to	Being mean, unkind, cruel, or unflattering	Smile: acknowledge the presence of other people and take time to listen to them.
Courtesy	Treating other people with respect, recognizing that all are made in God's image and likeness	Not recognizing the inherent dignity of others made in God's image and likeness	Be aware of others' feelings and expressions; be polite, well-mannered.
Generosity	Giving of oneself in a willing and cheerful manner for the good of others	Giving without a spirit of cheer, with a begrudging manner	Be self-giving; focus on one act of charity/kindness each day; share.
Gratitude	Thankful disposition of mind and heart	Not expressing appreciation; taking other people and things for granted	Count the good things (blessings) in one's life; express gratitude even when it is difficult.
Kindness	Expressing genuine concern about the well-being of others; anticipating their needs	Not regarding the well-being of others, being cruel in looks, words, and actions	Practice speaking, thinking, and acting kindly.
Loyalty	Accepting the bonds implicit in relationships and defending the virtues upheld by Church, family, and country	Breaking bonds of trust with Church, family, country, friends, and school	Seek to do one's best to help others; follow rules; fulfill responsibilities; be faithful to commitments.
Obedience	Assenting to rightful authority without hesitation or resistance	Resisting the directives of rightful authority	Seek to do one's best to help others; follow rules; fulfill responsibilities; be faithful to commitments.
Patriotism	Paying due honor and respect to one's country, with a willingness to serve	Lacking regard or respect for one's country and national symbols	Show respect for your country's flag; speak respectfully about government officials; recite the Pledge.
Prayerfulness	Being still, listening, and being willing to talk to God as a friend	Entertaining distractions during prayers and Mass	Cultivate a spirit of prayer and recollection; maintain the proper posture (kneeling, sitting still, etc.).
Respect	Speaking and acting according to one's own and others' rights, status, and circumstances	Resisting the directives of rightful authority	Be respectful in words and actions (body language); allow others to go first.
Responsibility	Fulfilling one's just duties; accepting the consequences of one's words and actions, intentional and unintentional	Failing to accept responsibility for one's words and/or actions; being unreliable	Be accountable for one's personal actions and decisions at home, at school, and in personal relationships.
Sincerity	Trustfulness in words and actions; honesty and enthusiasm toward others	Speaking or acting in a manner only to make oneself look good; being insincere	Tell the whole truth; build trust by words and actions; state what one is sorry for.
Trustworthiness	Acting in a way that inspires confidence and trust; being reliable	Being devious or deceptive	Perform actions that restore and maintain trust; act with fidelity in small matters.

VIRTUE	MEANING	OPPOSING TRAIT	WAYS TO CULTIVATE
PRUDENCE (Sound Judgment)	Enables one to reason and to act rightly in any given situation — "right reason in action"	Being hasty or rash in one's words or actions	Pray for guidance. Seek sound advice. Think about the situation. Act upon the decision.
PARTS OF A PRUDENTIAL ACT			
Good Counsel — Ask and listen	Seeking advice from a reasonable person	Seeking advice from those who agree with you; asking moral advice from people who do not share your moral values	Seek advice from trustworthy people.
Good Judgment — Think	Thinking rightly about a decision	Acting without thinking	Carefully consider all the circumstances and ask "What am I to do now?"
Command — Act	Directly acting upon a sound decision	Failing to act upon a sound decision	Take action after thoughtful deliberation
VIRTUES			
Circumspection	Careful consideration of circumstances and consequences	Considering only oneself when acting	Seek advice silently reflect upon the circumstances and consequences of one's actions (memory).
Docility	Willingness to be taught	Being stubborn, inflexible, and proudly set in one's ways	Listen to others and be willing to follow directions; thank others for rightful corrections.
Foresight	Consideration of the consequences of one's actions; thinking ahead	Failing to consider later consequences	Pray, think, act; learn how to gather information to make a decision; plan out long-term and short-term goals.
FORTITUDE (Courage)	Enables one to endure difficulties and pain for the sake of what is good	Choosing the easiest task; being cowardly; being insensible to fear	Withstand difficulties; complete hard tasks.
Industriousness	Diligence, especially in work that leads to natural and supernatural maturity	Choosing the easiest task; being cowardly; being insensible to fear	Diligently complete a task; set small goals along the way.
Magnanimity	Seeking with confidence to do great things in God; literally "having a large soul"	Giving in to a lack of motivation to complete one's responsibilities; being lazy	Acknowledge the good in others when it is difficult; strive to do difficult tasks with God's grace.
Magnificence	Doing great things for God	Giving in to a lack of motivation to complete one's responsibilities; being lazy	Use one's talents for the good; act with generosity toward others.
Patience	Bearing present difficulties calmly	Being impatient while completing a difficult task or in handling challenging circumstances	Listen to others; wait for one's turn; tolerate inconveniences and annoyances without complaining.
Perseverance	Taking the steps necessary to carry out objectives in spite of difficulties	Quickly giving up when a task is challenging	Complete task from start to finish; stay with a task when it is hard, difficult, or boring.
TEMPERANCE (Self-Control)	Sincerity, openness and truthfulness in one's words and actions	Being dishonest in words and actions; telling lies	Live uprightly in words and actions; recognize that "God sees the heart".
Honesty	Enables one to be moderate in the pleasure and use of created goods	Intemperance; overindulging in a good thing	Exercise the freedom to say 'no' to one's wants and desires.
Humility	Awareness that all one's gifts come from God and appreciation for the gifts of others	Failing to recognize the gifts of others; being too proud or having false humility	Show deference to others; acknowledge the accomplishments of others; look at one's strengths and weaknesses honestly.
Meekness	Serenity of spirit while focusing on the needs of others	Giving in to anger and losing one's temper when working or playing with others	Remain calm; allow others to go first; wait without complaining.
Moderation	Attention to balance in one's life	Giving in to being excessive in one or more areas of one's life	Set limits for oneself; create a balance in one's life by limiting the use of media, consumption of additional food and drink, etc.
Modesty	Purity of heart in action, especially in regards to dress and speech	Choosing to dress or act in a way inconsistent with one's dignity as a child of God	Follow the dress code; recognize your dignity as a person; ask yourself if you are respecting yourself as a child of God.
Orderliness	Keeping oneself physically clean and neat and one's belongings in good order	Disorder with regard to one's space and physical appearance	Establish order in one's daily life; keep one's space and appearance orderly and clean.
Self-Control	Joyful mastery over one's passions and desires	Being excessive in words or actions, acting impulsively	Mastery of one's desires; practice restraint in regards to words and actions

Section 4 | How to Educate in Virtue?

Educating the young in virtue is a process, a gradual growth in virtue. We can frame the education in three stages: Learn, Live, and Witness.

Learn, Live, Witness

As Catholic educators, we have the privilege and task to guide young disciples in the Christian life. Everything in the classroom and the school is formative. It is through individual formation of each child that he or she is able to see himself and the world through God's eyes, and to act as God would have him act at all times. The goal—of education, of discipline, of formation—is true cultivation of virtue so that each child is interiorly directed away from patterns of behavior that are in need of change and toward God Himself. All instruction in the life of virtue and classroom discipline plans should therefore be rooted in recognizing the dignity of each person.

Educating the young in virtue is a process, a gradual growth in virtue. We can frame the education in three stages: Learn, Live, and Witness.

LEARN WAYS TO PRACTICE VIRTUE,
LIVE JOYFULLY AS A DISCIPLE OF CHRIST,
WITNESS CONVERSION AND HAPPINESS.

In the beginning stages, we want the students to learn the language of virtue. Virtues are the habits of doing good, so we show them the specific actions, words, and behaviors that are virtuous. We teach them what virtue is, what it "looks like" and "sounds like." When each child was created, God planted in his or her heart the desire for goodness. He then gave each child the virtues and gifts of the Holy Spirit at Baptism. Our task as educators is to help draw out this virtue, to help the child identify and practice it in his or her life.

When you incorporate the language of virtue into your classroom routines, you are able to do two things. Your routines become catechetical, teaching students about the virtues. It also transforms your discipline into an approach that is positive and virtue building.

LEARN — WAYS TO PRACTICE VIRTUE

—LEARN WAYS TO PRACTICE VIRTUE—

- Use the virtue cards for whole class instruction on individual virtues.
- Create a virtue center in your classroom.
- Structure your classroom routines and classroom management around the virtues.
- Have a virtue of the week. On Monday teach that virtue. Throughout the week, have the students watch for ways their classmates practice that virtue. When a student is "caught" practicing virtue, have some simple way of celebrating that success.
- Use the language of virtue in your classroom rules or expectations. Instead of "Don't speak without raising your hand," say, "Practice self-control by raising your hand if you want to speak."
- Frame discipline conversations around the virtues. Instead of a "don't do that again approach," turn them in to teaching opportunities and empower your students by sharing with them virtues they can practice and ways they can handle similar situations differently in the future.

Learn, Live, Witness

LIVE
AS A DISCIPLE OF CHRIST

As the students learn the language of the virtues, they are able to live them out in their daily lives. In learning the virtues, students learn the characteristics of a good, integrated life. Students are properly empowered to act virtuously in daily situations—at home and at school, on the playground, on the sports field. This may manifest itself by reaching out in kindness to a lonely student, being courageous by standing up for another, or persevering through seemingly endless homework.

WITNESS
CONVERSION AND HAPPINESS

The virtuous life is a happy life because it is integrated, freed from the disorder of conflicting emotions and desires. The disciple is able to live in friendship with Christ, Who is our fulfillment and hope. The disciple has the *habitus* of virtue. This is more than just a habit. Habits are routine, almost thoughtless because they are automatic. One can perform habits while thinking about something else, like brushing your teeth while mentally planning your day. But a *habitus* is dynamic and operative, meaning that the virtue has become second nature, so firmly rooted in us, we can act easily in the good. The overflow of these good actions is joy, giving the disciple delight in doing good.

—LIVE AS A DISCIPLE OF CHRIST—

- When doing character study in language arts or discussing historical persons, use the language of virtues and vices.
- As students and teachers see others practicing virtue, have a way that that can be recognized and celebrated. Give out virtue certificates, have a "caught practicing virtue" bulletin board, or send an email home to the parents.
- At some point during the day, do a "virtue checkpoint." Ask the students to think about their day in light of a particular virtue. Have they practiced it? When? Where should they have practiced it? Then, say a prayer together, asking God for the grace to be virtuous.

—WITNESS CONVERSION AND HAPPINESS—

- Incorporate regular and intentional times of silence in your school schedule. Practice various forms of prayer together as a class, such as *lectio divina*, praying the rosary, or Eucharistic adoration.
- Cultivate a Catholic culture in your classroom and school. This can be done by creating sacred spaces, regular times and places of prayer, and displaying sacred art in the building. Encourage the practice of virtue, and create an environment where virtue is easy.
- Use Christian witness certificates to point out and encourage students who regularly practice a specific virtue.

Living Virtuously Is Discipline

The Life of Saint John Bosco

- BORN IN 1815, BECCHI, ITALY
- DIED JANUARY 31, 1888 IN TURIN, ITALY
- FOUNDER OF THE SALESIAN SOCIETY
- DEVELOPED *THE PREVENTATIVE SYSTEM*
- BUILT SEVERAL BASILICAS
- BY THE TIME HE DIED IN 1888, THERE WERE 250 HOUSES OF THE SALESIAN SOCIETY IN THE WORLD
- HE IS THE MODEL FOR ALL EDUCATORS, AND SCHOOL CHILDREN
- MOTTO: "GIVE ME SOULS AND TAKE AWAY THE REST"
- FEAST DAY: JANUARY 31

Creating a Discipline Plan Based on the Virtues

True discipline is nothing more than Christian formation by which educators assist children to become disciples of Christ. The guiding principles of a discipline plan based on the virtues stem from the three main elements of St. John Bosco's *Preventive System in the Education of Youth*: reason, religion, and kindness. The term *preventive* is derived from the Latin verb *praevenire*; that is, to "foresee" and "provide." Familiarity and kindness, gentle presence, open dialogue, and willing cooperation mark this style, all of which point to a virtuous system.

- **Reason:** When both the "reason" and the "rule" is shared with students, they can better know that these expectations are in place to help them act like disciples. Appealing to a child's reason respects his or her dignity and allows the child to be brought into the decision-making experience, allowing him or her to take ownership and responsibility.

- **Religion:** "God gives the growth" (1 Corinthians 3:7). This is good news—especially for the child struggling with a specific behavior. Keeping this in the forefront of all discipline conversations helps make the child realize that practicing virtue—or learning how to raise your hand before speaking—is not an insurmountable task. Most importantly, pray with your students, right there, in the midst of the discipline conversation.

- **Kindness:** All correction must be wrapped in kindness. Practically, that means it should be "sandwiched" in between real and concrete praise for the child. The child needs to hear from you that he or she is loved and valued and that you have hope in him or her. Sometimes, this may mean delaying the conversation until the appropriate time.

Disciple of Christ: Living Virtuously Is Discipline

Nothing replaces the value of personal witness. Students can learn to respond to their teachers, their peers, and to their own inner desires in a virtuous manner if they see these good habits employed by all members of the faculty in a spirit of loving presence and constant availability.

St. John Bosco understood that youth can be, at times, thoughtless and irresponsible. Modern psychological studies explain why: their frontal lobes—the region in the brain for decision making, impulse control, attention—may not be fully developed until the mid twenties. However, rather than enforcing a stringent discipline of corporal and verbal punishments which insinuate negativity, Bosco believed the teacher would reach far more deeply into the souls of the young and affect the good by applying reason, religion, and kindness.

Because it is in stressful moments that one's virtue is most tested, faculty and staff should seek to incorporate elements from the *Preventive System* when correcting a student and thus also guide his understanding of wrongdoing and his decisions toward the proper virtuous response. Teachers should always strive to keep in mind the dignity of the child and thus to correct in truth and love.

When a student's behavior is inconsistent with the expectations set forth in the school and/or classroom policies, the first response should be to assist the student in recognizing the behavior which needs to change. This can take place by a simple glance, a gentle tap on the shoulder, quietly saying the student's name, or if necessary, a brief conversation. Extreme care should be taken not to embarrass or demoralize the child.

Keeping in mind that an effective discipline plan provides an atmosphere of harmony and the freedom to respond to God's grace and love, teachers should instruct students in the academic disciplines while giving each the opportunity to develop and flourish as a child of God. All discipline should have as its aim the counseling, encouraging, and aiding of each young person toward the unique fulfillment of his/her fullest growth and maturity.

Often educators are good at assisting students to recognize inappropriate behavior. Incorporating the virtues into a discipline plan helps provide students with a way out of that behavior, especially if it has become a pattern. Ending discipline conversations with a virtue to practice and ways to pray for its increase gives students something concrete they can do. Instead of focusing on what *not* to do, focus instead on what to do. If a child keeps blurting out answers in class, have a conversation about

why he is doing that. Maybe he is so engaged it is exciting for him; maybe he talks without thinking. You could talk about a few virtues—maybe self-control, patience, or docility. Say a prayer together to the Holy Spirit and let the child pick a virtue. Together, talk about ways to cultivate that virtue—what it "looks like" and "sounds like." Then, in the next few days and weeks, watch for signs of that virtue, and celebrate each attempt. It may be a little bit before "success," but we are not after perfection, at least not on this earth. This life of discipleship is a journey; we are always growing and striving. Our task as educators is to mentor young disciples as they make the steps to follow in the footsteps of Christ.

Disciple of Christ: Living Virtuously is Discipline

PRACTICAL TOOLS FOR EDUCATORS

The purpose of discipline is to guide the child to a change in behavior—to move from a negative to a positive. By using the language of the virtues, the educator is better able to persuade the child to strive for goodness.

Teachers

Practically speaking, it takes more time to use the *Preventive System* by St. John Bosco for discipline.

As teachers/educators, we should always be living in the spirit of a witness to the children. Before engaging a student in a discipline conversation, ask yourself these questions:

Self-Check:

- Are you angry, tired, or frustrated?
- Have you clearly communicated your classroom discipline plan and expectations? Do you have a classroom discipline plan?
- Do you wait too long before enforcing your discipline plan?
- What tone of voice are you using when speaking to the child(ren)? Are you communicating gentleness with firmness?
- Are you present to the children? (Or focused on grading papers and getting other "stuff" done?)
- Are you focused more on enforcing the rules as opposed to helping the students understand "why" they need to change their behavior?
- Do you allow the child the time and space to explain their perspective? *(See Student section.)*

Conferencing with the student:

- **Schedule a time to talk personally with the child to explain why his/her behavior needs to be changed.** *(Note that this conversation should begin with the child knowing that you genuinely care about him/her as a person.)*
- During the conversation, allow the child/student to communicate their perspective *(See student section below).*
- Discuss positive virtues you already recognize in the student.
- Make a plan on how you will work together to improve their behavior by working on virtues that were lacking.

Communication

- Communicate the plan with the (1) principal, (2) co-workers, and (3) parents.

Implementation

- Implement the plan.

Students

Self-reflection, or "think sheets," are a useful tool in establishing a discipline plan. Allowing the child/student to use the method of self-reflection eases the burden from the teacher and puts the responsibility on the student to understand their poor choice and reflect or "think" about what he/she could have done better. "Think Sheets" should be created differently based on the age level, but should convey the following self-reflection questions:

- The poor choice I made was…
- I made this choice because…
- A better choice would be to…
- The virtue(s) I should practice is/are…
- This virtue would "look like" and "sound like"…

Disciple of Christ: Living Virtuously is Discipline

EXAMPLES OF SELF-REFLECTION OR "THINK SHEETS"

Note about "Action Taken" section:

Due to the increase of passivity in the culture, consequences such as sitting quietly for a period of time are generally not corrective and may not address the needed change in attitude or behavior. Students tend to think concretely and therefore, the action taken should be an active consequence that is corrective and restorative.

Disciple of Christ: Living Virtuously is Discipline

DISCIPLE OF CHRIST REPORT

Since the first school of discipline is the home, it is imperative that educators seek to establish and maintain close communication with parents. The following are suggested means of communication related to student development and discipline:

The *Disciple of Christ* report is an effective means to communicate individual adherence to the discipline plan of the school and/or classroom. It serves as a positive tool to acknowledge virtuous behavior and to further the confidence of each child. The contents and frequency of the report may vary according to the age level. It is the goal that each child will recognize the call to be a disciple of Christ rooted in the daily living of the gospel.

The Disciple of Christ Report has two components shown below which can be used in conjunction with any code of conduct and discipline policy in a school. They can also be used as part of a behavioral modification plan.

CHRISTIAN WITNESS CERTIFICATE

The Christian Witness Certificate acknowledges a student who has exemplified Christian virtue.

DISCIPLE OF CHRIST REPORT

The Disciple of Christ Report helps a student identify a virtue he/she needs to cultivate. Including "suggested ways to cultivate" by listing concrete examples helps dispose the student to God's grace while developing good habits.

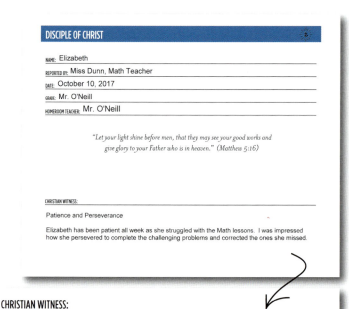

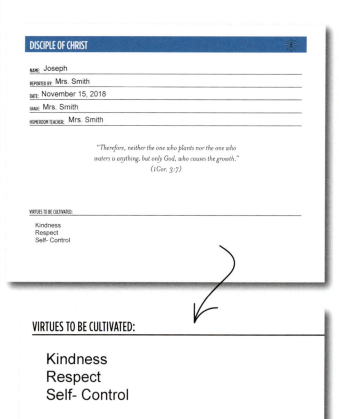

"Neither he who plants nor he who waters is anything, but only God gives the growth." (1 Corinthians. 3:7)

Resources

Use the following resources to develop the lexicon, or language, in your home or school. Learning the language is the first stage and the foundation of virtue education. The following resources will help educators and students identify and understand the virtues, gifts of the Holy Spirit, etc.

EDUCATOR'S GUIDE

The *Educator's Guide* opens with overview of the theological and moral virtues, the call to holiness, and the rationale of the curriculum. It is imperative that parents and educators be convinced that everyone is called to be a disciple of Christ, and that through a personal encounter with Him, one is gifted with interior happiness and freedom.

For each virtue, there is a resource page that includes: meaning of the virtue, opposing trait, age appropriate ways to cultivate, Scripture passages, examples from the lives of the saints, and prayer. The virtue cards, saint cards, and instructional posters all align with the *Educator's Guide*, making this a one-stop spot for lesson planning.

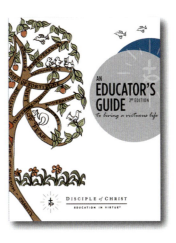

DISCIPLE OF CHRIST VIRTUE CHART

The Disciple of Christ Virtue Chart enables the parent, instructor or student to become familiar with the virtues. This chart features a list of the virtues in their respective color-coded cardinal virtue, and includes the virtue meanings, opposing trait, and ways to cultivate.

Use this chart to:

- Easily identify the virtue meaning, opposing trait, and ways to cultivate the virtue
- Identify age level virtue suggestions for practical and concrete ways to cultivate growth in a virtue
- Provide a common vocabulary among educators, parents, and students

**11" X 17" SIZE / 2-SIDED / FOLDED / LAMINATED
(SOLD AS PART OF THE VIRTUE CHART PACK)**

See full-size charts, pages 138–139

REMAIN IN ME CHART

This easy-to-use, two-sided chart gives you and your students or children an overview of the theological virtues, the cardinal virtues, the gifts of the Holy Spirit, and the fruits of the Holy Spirit. Turn the chart over to see the Virtue Tree (right), which provides a visual of how the virtues are interconnected and how the gifts are related to the virtues.

**8.5" X 11" SIZE / 2-SIDED / LAMINATED
(SOLD AS PART OF THE VIRTUE CHART PACK)**

Resources: Learn, Live, Witness

VIRTUE CARDS

The virtue cards are essential in helping students learn how to practice virtue. The color-coded cards feature an image and example of what that virtue "looks like" and "sounds like." There are 8-12 cards for every virtue so that students can learn practical ways to practice it. The back of the card includes a prayer, saint picture and biography, and Scripture passage.

Use these cards to:

- Highlight a particular virtue that needs to be cultivated in group or individual behavior
- Identify virtuous behavior
- Modify classroom behavior
- Model virtuous behavior through role play
- Have students select a personal virtue and come up with concrete ways of practicing it for a week!

LARGE VIRTUE CARDS - 6.5" X 9" INSTRUCTIONAL USE
SMALL VIRTUE CARDS - 4.25" X 5.5" STUDENT USE

Using a Virtue Card for Behavior Modification

Display cards which show the behavior that needs modification. The student will select a card which coincides with the virtue in need of cultivation. For example, if a child is playing too rough on the playground, the teacher could display the Meekness, Self-Control, or Kindness virtue card.

DISCIPLE OF CHRIST—EDUCATION IN VIRTUE MINI-SERIES DVD

What are the virtues? And how can we learn to live them at any age?

After being asked to share their experience and practical tools for teaching and imparting a plan to bring the virtues to the wider population, the Dominican Sisters of Mary, Mother of the Eucharist, have created *Disciple of Christ, Education in Virtue: Mini-Series*.

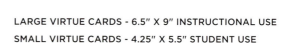

Includes appearances from: Most Rev. Thomas Olmsted, Bishop of the Roman Catholic Diocese of Phoenix; Most Rev. Earl Boyea, Bishop of the Roman Catholic Diocese of Lansing; Mother Assumpta Long, OP; Teresa Tomeo; Deacon Larry Oney; Tom Monaghan, and many more!

As seen on EWTN. 1 Disc / 2 Hours

Series includes episodes covering:

- *Happiness is Living a Virtuous Life*. The life of virtue equips one to strive for happiness while pursuing the good.
- *Foundation for Moral Formation in Character*. Educating in virtue is essential for character formation and living a life of freedom and grace.
- *Theological and Moral Virtues*. At Baptism God gives us the seed of eternal life. By cooperating with His grace, the Christian can experience the fullness of the theological and cardinal virtues, as well as the gifts of the Holy Spirit.
- *Cultivating Virtue to Battle Sin*. A life of virtue gives one the ability to break the pattern of sin and enables one to experience harmony in one's life.
- *Lectio Divina*. Through a prayerful reading of Scripture, the disciple is able to hear the voice of Christ the Teacher and follow Him.
- *How to Teach Virtue*. This segment offers best practices in classroom strategies from experienced educators about how to educate students and youth in virtue.
- *Culture of Virtue*. Listen to different teachers, parents, and administrators explain how a culture of virtue enhances the Catholic identity of the school.

Resources: Learn, Live, Witness

WAYS TO CULTIVATE POSTER

With blank space to write in ways to cultivate a particular virtue, instructors or parents can assess if children understand the virtue, as well as create opportunities to highlight virtuous behavior modeled in the classroom.

Put up several posters, and with the use of dry-erase markers, have students brainstorm new ideas every week.

SOLD IN COMPLETE SETS OF 28 POSTERS TOTAL

11" X 17" SIZE / 1-SIDED / DRY ERASE

INSTRUCTIONAL POSTERS

The Instructional Poster series includes one large instructional poster for each of the virtues. The posters are color-coded to their respective cardinal virtue.

SOLD IN COMPLETE SETS OF 28 POSTERS TOTAL

The front of each virtue poster features:

- The virtue and its meaning
- Images that demonstrate the "looks like" and "sounds like" aspect of the virtue
- Related cardinal virtue
- Corresponding gift of the Holy Spirit
- Prayer

For ease of use while holding the poster during instruction, the back side of the poster includes:

- The related cardinal virtue and gift of the holy spirit with definitions
- The opposing trait and its meaning
- Brief biographies of several saints
- Scripture references

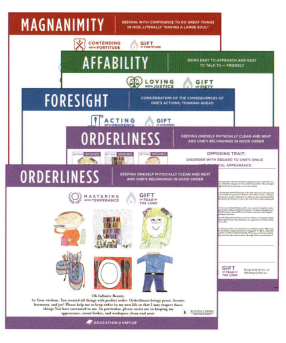

18" X 24" SIZE / 2-SIDED / LAMINATED

"LOOKS LIKE," "SOUND LIKE" POSTER

Want to check for understanding? After an instruction in a specific virtue, a teacher or student can demonstrate what a virtue "Looks Like" and "Sounds Like."

18" X 24" SIZE / ONE-SIDED / DRY ERASE

151

Resources: Learn Live, Witness

SAINT CARDS

These holy cards are reminders of a particular virtue to cultivate. Small enough to carry in one's pocket, these cards feature an image of the saint, a prayer to help acquire the virtue, the definition of that virtue, and a Scripture passage.

Saint cards are available in:

- Complete sets (variety) each saint card set contains one unique saint card per virtue for a total of 35 cards
- Packs (same card) saint card packs contain 48 of the same saint card

Suggested ways to use the Saint Cards

- Start a Saint Card collection.
- Reward a student who demonstrates the virtue.
- Give to a student to help cultivate a certain virtue.
- Distribute to an entire class.
- Select a saint card from a basket and cultivate the virtue.

CARD SIZE 2.75" X 4.25" / TWO-SIDED

VIRTUE TREE POSTER

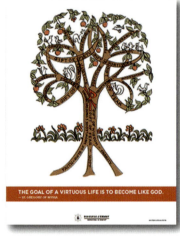

The Virtue Tree Poster is an instructional tool that identifies how the virtues are organic and interrelated. Have children follow along with their finger to discover the unity of the virtues and the gifts of the Holy Spirit.

A great idea for a bulletin board!

18" X 24" SIZE / ONE-SIDED

WORKS OF MERCY COLORING BOOK

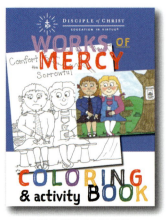

Bring some color into your child's life while learning about the works of mercy. Coloring our original artwork and completing the activity pages will help your students and children better understand how they can practice the Corporal and Spiritual Works of Mercy.

The perforated pages make it easy to share the joy of coloring with your children and to invite others to join you. Hang them on your refrigerator or in your classroom!

8.5" X 11" | 124 PAGES

Resources: Learn, Live, Witness

The first step to living as a disciple of Christ is to know the person of Jesus Christ. Use the following resources to allow your students/children to develop a relationship with Jesus by studying and reflecting on His word using *lectio divina*.

SNAPSHOT OF THE KERYGMA

Kerygma originally comes from a Greek word that means "proclamation." It is the proclamation of disciples, of those who have heard Christ, seen Him, touched Him (cf. 1 John 1:1) and have found their meaning, purpose, and identity in Him. The kerygma is the proclamation of all that God has done for our us. It is the Good News. This visual of God's loving plan of our salvation provides an understanding of the kerygmatic foundation of a life of virtue.

The snapshot of the Kerygma provides a visual for:

- The loving plan of God for us
- Sin and its devastating consequences, especially separation from God (visual broken vine)
- God's answer to our predicament in the sending of his Son for our salvation
- Our response (conversion, faith, sacramental living) to live a new life as a joyful disciple of Christ

8.5" X 11" SIZE / TWO-SIDED

LIFE OF CHRIST, LECTIO DIVINA JOURNAL

The *Life of Christ, Lectio Divina Journal* was written to allow you to have an encounter with the Person of Jesus Christ. As you journey through the life of Christ by reading the selected scripture passages, you will slowly move through His life, meditating upon His word using *lectio divina*. This encounter with truth, beauty, and goodness, will show you how a life of virtue becomes an interior habit, a way of life, which enables you to be more open to the Holy Spirit, allowing you to make your own personal commitment to live as a disciple of Christ. Includes over **seventy-five religious art images!**

Suggested uses for the *Life of Christ, Lectio Divina Journal*:

- Use the life of Christ over a twoyear time period with students in the 7th–8th grade as a tool for confirmation preparation
- Use with high school students to allow time to meditate on the Word of God

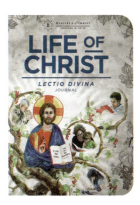

TITLE: *LIFE OF CHRIST, LECTIO DIVINA JOURNAL*
SIZE: 7.5" X 10.75"
NUMBER OF PAGES: 326

Resources: Learn, *Live*, Witness

SEASONAL *LECTIO DIVINA* JOURNALS

Journals for the liturgical seasons of Lent and Advent are offered to help you encounter the person of Jesus Christ. All of the journals include scripture readings, beautiful religious art images as well as questions to allow one to meditate on the Word using *lectio divina*. Below are two examples. Recommended for students in grades 5-8 as well as high school and up.

TITLE: ADVENT JOURNAL, MOTHER OF LIFE
SIZE: 6" X 9"
NUMBER OF PAGES: 104

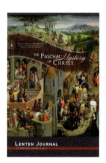

TITLE: LENTEN JOURNAL, THE PASCHAL MYSTERY OF CHRIST
SIZE: 6" X 9"
NUMBER OF PAGES: 136

LECTIO DIVINA JOURNALS / RESOURCES

A variety of journals are offered to help you encounter the person of Jesus Christ. Some journals have a theme to study more deeply a subject such as *The Word became Flesh* which studies the 4 reasons for the Incarnation or *The Disciple of Mercy Journal*, which focuses on the Works of Mercy. All of the journals include Scripture readings, beautiful religious art images as well as questions to allow one to meditate on the Word using *lectio divina*.

TITLE: DISCIPLE OF MERCY JOURNAL
SIZE: 8.5" X 11"
NUMBER OF PAGES: 140

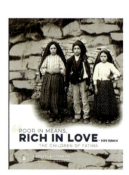

TITLE: RICH IN LOVE THE CHILDREN OF FATIMA
SIZE: 8.5" X 11"
NUMBER OF PAGES: 40

TITLE: AND THE WORD BECAME FLESH JOURNAL
SIZE: 8.5" X 11"
NUMBER OF PAGES: 60

Resources: Learn, Live, Witness

RINGS AND NECKLACE

The titanium medals and stamped ring with the Cross and Icthus logo will be a daily visible reminder to live the life of virtue as a disciple of Christ. Hand–stamped with the logo on the front of the ring and the inscription of Mt. 5:16 on the inside, every student and adult will cherish their ring for years to come!

"Let your light so shine before men, that they may see your good works and give glory to your Father who is in heaven." —Matthew 5:16

HAPPINESS IS PAMPHLET

Who am I? Where am I going? How do I find happiness? These are the questions that every person asks. Jesus Christ holds the answer and calls us to experience freedom and joy by living as His disciple. This pamphlet proposes an examination of conscience under this schema of discipleship. We find happiness by following Christ in a life of virtue.

Suggested uses for the *Happiness Is Living a Virtuous Life* Pamphlet:

- Use this virtue-based examen to identify the virtues you need to cultivate along your path of conversion.

4.67" X 8.5" SIZE / TRI-FOLD
(SOLD AS PART OF THE VIRTUE CHART PACK)

SAINT CARDS

These small holy cards are reminders of a particular virtue to cultivate. Easy enough to carry in one's pocket, these cards feature an image of the Saint, a prayer to help acquire the virtue, the definition of that virtue, and a Scripture passage.

Saint cards are available in:

- Complete sets (variety) each saint card set contains 1 unique saint card per virtue for a total of 35 cards
- Packs (same card) — saint card packs contain 48 of the same saint card

CARD SIZE 2.75" X 4.25" / TWO-SIDED

Resources: Learn, Live, Witness

When His love is the foundation of your identity and worth, you are free to love Him in return. To be a disciple of Christ means to love God above all things and your neighbor as yourself. Practicing the works of mercy is a concrete way to show your love of God and neighbor. Be a witness and reach out to others by virtuously living the Spiritual and Corporal Works of Mercy.

All of us are invited to "go out" as missionary disciples, each generously offering their talents, creativity, wisdom, and experience in order to bring the message of God's tenderness and compassion to the entire human family. —Pope Francis

CORPORAL WORKS OF MERCY

- † **GIVE FOOD TO THE HUNGRY:** Making a personal sacrifice to nourish another person's body and soul
- † **GIVE DRINK TO THE THIRSTY:** Giving others refreshment to sustain their physical and spiritual life
- † **CLOTHE THE NAKED:** Aiding others in recognizing the dignity of their bodies by treating them in a manner that expresses this dignity
- † **SHELTER THE HOMELESS:** Welcoming others and making them feel at home; giving them an experience of kindness and security
- † **VISIT THE SICK:** Supporting those bearing Christ's cross with your prayer and presence
- † **VISIT THE IMPRISONED:** Reaching out through prayer and kind support to those in prison or who have less freedom
- † **BURY THE DEAD:** Laying to rest the body of someone who has died and helping their loved ones grieve

SPIRITUAL WORKS OF MERCY

- † **TEACHING THE IGNORANT:** Teaching others the knowledge they need to be happy and fulfilled in this life and in the next
- † **COUNSEL THE DOUBTFUL:** Bringing peace of mind to another through good advice and uplifting words and deeds
- † **ADMONISH THE SINNER:** Calling others to conversion and encouraging them in pursuit of holiness
- † **BEAR WRONGS PATIENTLY:** Receiving slights, insults, and inconveniences cheerfully and without judging or expressing irritation
- † **FORGIVE OFFENSES:** Extending God's merciful love to someone who has hurt you, and letting go of his or her guilt
- † **COMFORT THE SORROWFUL:** Lightening another's burden of sorrow through care and compassion
- † **PRAY FOR THE LIVING AND THE DEAD:** Loving your neighbor as yourself through interceding for the needs of all

Resources: Learn, Live, Witness

ONLINE RESOURCES

Visit our Educator's Page on www.educationinvirtue.com for more information and ideas on how to implement the program. We have free materials and post ideas and share information on a periodic basis. Also, follow us on Pinterest, Facebook or Twitter to receive the latest news from Education in Virtue.

Find us on:

WEBSITE: WWW.EDUCATIONINVIRTUE.COM
PINTEREST @EDUINVIRTUE
TWITTER @EDUINVIRTUE
FACEBOOK @EDUCATIONINVIRTUE

BULLETIN BOARDS
IDEAS
VIRTUE OF THE WEEK
FREE PRINTABLES
ARTICLES
VIDEOS
SAINT OF THE DAY

Resources: For Further Reading

Aristotle. *The Nicomachean Ethics*. Translated by David Ross. New York: Oxford University Press Inc., 1998

Aumann, Jordan, OP and Royo, Antonio, OP. *The Theology of Christian Perfection*. Iowa: The Priory Press, 1962

Avallone, Paul, S.D.B. *Key to the Hearts of Youth*. New Rochelle, New York: Salesiana Publishers, 1999. *Catechism of the Catholic Church*. 2nd Ed. Vatican: Libreria Edetricia Vaticana, 1997

Cessario, Romanus, OP. *Christian Faith and the Theological Life*. Washington, D.C.: Catholic University of America Press, 1996

Cessario, Romanus, OP. *The Moral Virtues and Theological Ethics*. 2nd Ed. Indiana: University of Notre Dame Press, 2009

Cessario, Romanus, OP. *The Virtues or the Examined Life*. New York: Continuum International Publishing Group Inc., 2002

Farrell, Walter, OP. *Companion to the Summa (Vol. 1–4)*. London: Sheed and Ward, 1938

Farrell, Walter, OP and Healy, Martin J., STD. *My Way of Life: Pocket Edition of St. Thomas, The Summa Simplified for Everyone*. New York: Confraternity of the Precious Blood, 1952

Glenn, Msgr. Paul. *A Tour of the Summa*. Illinois: Tan Books, 1960

Kaczor, Christopher and Sherman, Thomas, SJ. *Thomas Aquinas on the Cardinal Virtues*. Florida: Ave Maria University Press, 2009

Kaczor, Christopher. *Thomas Aquinas on Faith, Hope, and Love*. Florida: Ave Maria University Press, 2008

Morgan, Barbara. *Echoing the Mystery*. Michigan: Lumen Ecclesiae Press, 2018

Pieper, Joseph. *Faith, Hope, Love*. San Francisco: Ignatius Press, 1997

Pieper, Joseph. *The Four Cardinal Virtues*. Indiana: University of Notre Dame Press, 1966

Pinckaers, Servais, OP. *Morality: The Catholic View*. Translated by Michael Sherwin, OP. Indiana: St. Augustines Press, 2003

Pinckaers, Servais, OP. *The Pursuit of Happiness—God's Way*. Translated by Sr. Mary Thomas Noble, OP. New York: Alba House, 1998

Pinckaers, Servais, OP. *The Sources of Christian Ethics*. Translated by Sr. Mary Thomas Noble, OP. Washington, D.C.: Catholic University of America Press, 1995

Pope Benedict XVI. *Caritas in Veritate*. San Francisco: Ignatius Press, 2009

Pope Benedict XVI. *Deus Caritas Est*. San Francisco: Ignatius Press, 2006

Pope Benedict XVI. *Spe Salvi*. San Francisco: Ignatius Press, 2008

Pope Francis. *Lumen Fidei*. San Francisco: Ignatius Press, 2013

Thomas Aquinas, St. *Aquinas' Shorter Summa*. Translated by Cyril Vollert, SJ, New Hampshire: Sophia Institute Press, 1993

Thomas Aquinas, St. *The Cardinal Virtues*. Edited and Translated by Richard J. Regan. Indiana: Hackett Publishing, 2005

Thomas Aquinas, St. *The Summa Theologica*. Translated by the Fathers of the English Dominican Province. New York: Benziger Bros., 1947

Thomas Aquinas, St. *Summa Theologiae: A Concise Translation*. Edited by Timothy McDermot. Indiana: Christian Classics, 1989

Mensing, Cyprian. *An Activity Analysis of the Four Cardinal Virtues: Suggested by the Writings of St. Thomas*. Phd Diss., Catholic University of America, 1929. (Reprinted by Kessinger Publishing)

Vogt, Emmerich, OP. *The Freedom to Love*. Minnesota: Mill City Press, 2012

Internet Resources

The Disciple of Christ – Education in Virtue. http://www.educationinvirtue.com

Catechism of the Catholic Church. http://www.vatican.va/archive/ENG0015/_INDEX.HTM Accessed July 9, 2013

Catholic Education Resource Center. http://catholiceducation.org/ Accessed July 9, 2013

New Advent. http://newadvent.org/ Accessed July 9, 2013

United States Conference of Catholic Bishops. http://usccb.org/ Accessed July 9, 2013

GLOSSARY

- A -

Actual Grace – God's interventions of grace, help, or inspiration in the daily moments of our lives. This grace is called "actual" because it inspires our actions.

Adoration – humble acknowledgment that one is the creature, standing before an infinite Creator.

- B -

Beatitude – the state of enjoying perfect fulfillment and happiness, especially the happiness of seeing God face to face in heaven. This supernatural beatitude is the goal of our whole life. Grace makes it possible for us to share this divine happiness, even here on earth, though imperfectly.

- C -

Capital Sins – also known as "deadly sins;" these seven sins are at the root of all sinful behavior. They are: pride, envy, anger, acedia (sloth), avarice (greed), gluttony, lust.

Cardinal Virtues – the human virtues of prudence, justice, fortitude, and temperance. These four virtues act as the "hinge" of the good life, bringing the harmony of order into each aspect of human life. They are both the workings of grace and of human effort.

Catechesis – the act of handing on of the Faith by systematic instruction.

Communion – an intimate sharing of life among persons, mutual self gift. The foundational and original communion is the communion of the Persons of the Trinity. Made in the image and likeness of the Triune God, human beings are made for communion with one another and with God. Communion between human beings and God is brought about by His free gift of grace given to us at Baptism.

Concupiscence – the inclination to sin. This effect of original sin is not removed by Baptism, darkening our intellects and weakening our wills. By the help of grace and the practice of virtue helps overcome concupiscence, restoring the harmony within ourselves.

- D -

Deposit of Faith – the content of Divine Revelation - all that has been revealed by God fully in Christ, entrusted to the Apostles, and delivered completely to the Church to handed down throughout all ages. Our response is faith.

Divinization or "Divine Adoption" – literally, "to make divine;" by divinization, God changes man's nature, making us capable of sharing His own life as God. This happens by grace.

- E -

Evil – a state of being deprived of some good, when that good ought to be present.

- F -

Freedom – the ability to choose what is good and right, according to truth. Freedom is liberating because we are created for goodness and truth.

- G -

Glory – the radiance of God's supreme perfection. We will share in God's glory in heaven.

Gospel – literally "Good News;" the proclamation of the wonderful works of God, by which He accomplishes our salvation in Jesus Christ.

Grace – our participation in God's life. It is the supernatural life of the soul. It is freely given, chiefly through the sacraments.

- H -

Happiness – the joyful state of fulfillment and full flourishing, intended by God and corresponding to the deepest desires of our hearts.

Heart – the mysterious center of one's person, where one makes decisions and enters into communion with God.

Heaven – "What eye has not seen, and ear has not heard, and what has not entered the human heart, what God has prepared for those who love him" (1 Corinthians 2:9). Those who die in God's grace and are purified live forever with Him. Their chief joy is to "see Him as He is" (1 John 3:2). They are fully alive in Christ and at the resurrection of the body will experience the joy of the Lord in both soul and body.

Hell – the state of eternal self-exclusion from God and from the blessed in heaven. It is freely chosen by those who refuse God's love during their earthly lives. After the resurrection of the body, the sufferings of hell will be both spiritual and physical.

Human Person – a personal being, created in the image and likeness of God, destined to share eternal life with Him. Human persons are composite beings made of both body and soul together, with an intellect and will and the capacity for communion with others. We are engendered persons, created male and female, both sharing in equal dignity and both called to happiness in God.

- I -

Incarnation – literally, "made flesh;" the mystery of the divine Person of the eternal Son uniting in time a human nature to Himself, so that he truly became man, like us in all things but sin.

Intellect – mind; the power by which a person knows truth.

Interiority – the quality of being inclined to reflection which is cultivated by taking time for communion with God in silence and to examine one's actions, motivations, and what is right and just.

GLOSSARY

- K -

Kerygma – originally from the Greek and used in the New Testament to describe the Apostles' first proclamation of the Gospel. This core message includes the following elements: 1) God's loving plan for our salvation; 2) our rejection by sin and its consequences; 3) God's answer to the problem of sin by sending His Son whose death heals us; 4) our response to the gift of grace offered in Jesus Christ—the call to repent, believe, and follow Jesus Christ as His disciple and member of His family, the Church.

- L -

Lectio Divina – literally "divine reading;" the prayerful reading and meditation on the Word of God in the Scripture. It includes the following elements: prayerful reading (*lectio*), meditating on the text (*meditatio*), praying with the text (*oratio*), spending time with the Lord (*contemplatio*), and being open to change based on the text (*actio*).

- M -

Magisterium – from the Latin *magister* "teacher;" the teaching authority of the Church to safeguard and interpret the Word of God for each generation.

Mortal Sin – a gravely sinful act by which one rejects the love of God, thus worthy of damnation if a person does not repent before death. A person is guilty of mortal sin when: 1) the action itself is gravely sinful and the person commits the action with 2) full knowledge and 3) full consent.

- N -

- O -

Original Holiness - the state of justice and harmony of Adam and Eve before the Fall. They experienced communion with God, interior harmony within themselves, perfect peace in their interactions with each other, and harmony with the rest of creation. By the effect of this grace, they were preserved from suffering and death.

Original Sin – the sin committed by Adam and Eve by which they rejected God and His grace for all their descendants. The term also refers to the inherited condition of all their descendants, who enter life deprived of grace and thus with with a weakened human nature.

- P -

Paschal Mystery – the Passion, Death, Resurrection, and Ascension of Jesus, by which He accomplished our salvation.

Penance – An act of sacrifice or good work aimed at turning our hearts toward God, giving exterior expression to interior contrition for sin, and making reparation to God for sin. In the sacrament of Penance sins are forgiven and we perform a penance as a means of sharing in the work of restoring the damage done by sin.

Person – a being capable of self-knowledge, self-possession and of entering into communion with others. God is a Trinity of three divine Persons. There are also angelic persons and human persons.

Prayer – The lifting of the mind and heart to God, spending time with Him in loving conversation. St. Therese described prayer as "a surge of the heart; it is a simple look turned toward heaven, it is a cry of recognition and of love, embracing both trial and joy" (*CCC*, 2558).

- R -

Revelation – God's self-disclosure, by which He makes Himself known to us and invites us to share in His life. In sharing Himself with us, He shares with us His life, His love, and His plan for our salvation. Revelation is made complete in Jesus Christ, who also, as perfect man, reveals the full glory of what it means to be human.

- S -

Sacrament – in its broadest form, a sacrament is a visible sign of invisible reality. There are seven specific sacraments which are signs, instituted by Christ and entrusted to the Church, which make present the grace they signify. The seven sacraments are: Baptism, Confirmation, Eucharist, Penance (Reconciliation, Confession), Anointing of the Sick, Matrimony, Holy Orders.

Sanctifying Grace – that grace that makes us like God, that divinizes us and elevates us to share in God's supernatural life. It is the grace that makes us holy.

Saint – A person in heaven. Canonized saints are those Christians whose lives can serve as a reliable guide in the life of holiness. The saints have shown in their lives heroic virtue and, after their death, have obtained two miracles through their intercession.

Scripture – the Word of God, written by human authors acting under the inspiration of the Holy Spirit, so that it is truly God's word to us.

Sin – a deliberate thought, word, deed, or omission that is an act against God and right reason. It is "missing the mark," either by choosing a lesser good over a higher good, following our own selfishness instead of God's love, or an outright rejection of what is good. At its core, all sin, even the smallest, is a rejection of God and His love.

- T -

Theological Virtues – the virtues of faith, hope and love, which give us the supernatural ability to enter into relationship with God as His adopted children. They have God as their origin, motive, and end.

Tradition – the Word of God, handed down from Christ to the Apostles, and from them to their successors, in its totality, throughout all generations.

- V -

Vice – a habit of repeated sin such that one is now inclined toward that sin. Vice is overcome by prayer and deliberate effort to acquire the virtue which is its opposite.

Virtue – a firm and habitual disposition achieved by repeated good acts and elevated by grace which makes it easy and enjoyable to do what is good.

- W -

Will – The power by which a person decides and loves, by which we cooperate with God or reject His plan of loving goodness.

IMAGE CREDITS

Cover art: *The Kerygma Tree*, © Sister Emmanuel, O.P., Dominican Sisters of Mary, Mother of the Eucharist

Page 29: *Two Blind Men at Jericho,* illustration from 'The Life of Our Lord Jesus Christ', 1886–96, Tissot, James Jacques Joseph (1836-1902) / Brooklyn Museum of Art, New York, USA / Purchased by Public Subscription / Bridgeman Images

Page 30: *Bishop Fulton Sheen,* Library of Congress, Wikimedia Commons, Public Domain

Page 33: ©www.bradi-barth.org, Bradi-Barth

Page 34: *Presentation in the Temple* www.bradi-barth.org, Bradi-Barth

Page 41: *The Eternal Father* (oil on canvas), Veronese, (Paolo Caliari) (1528-88) / Hospital Tavera, Toledo, Spain / Bridgeman Images

Page 42: *Portrait of Josephine Bakhita,* author unknown, Wikimedia Commons, Public Domain

Page 47: ©www.bradi-barth.org, Bradi-Barth

Page 53: *Crucifixion*, Giotto di Bondone, circa 1300, fresco from Scrovegni Chapel, Wikimedia Commons, Public Domain

Page 54: *Mother Teresa,* Wikimedia Commons, Public Domain

Page 57: ©www.bradi-barth.org, Bradi-Barth

Page 63: *The Wise and Foolish Virgins,* Charles Ricketts, oil on canvas, Wikimedia Commons, Public Domain

Page 64: *Bl. Stanley Rother,* Photo courtesy of the Archdiocese of Oklahoma City Archives

Page 68: ©www.bradi-barth.org, Bradi-Barth

Page 69: *Bl. Miguel Pro,* © Sister Mariana, O.P., Dominican Sisters of Mary, Mother of the Eucharist

Page 69: *St. John Baptist de la Salle,* Wikimedia Commons, Public Domain

Page 69: *St. Jane Frances de Chantal,* Wikimedia Commons, Public Domain

Page 69: *St. Edmund Campion,* by Johann Martin Lerch, Wikimedia Commons, Public Domain

Page 70: *St. Dominic Savio,* © Sister Mariana, O.P., Dominican Sisters of Mary, Mother of the Eucharist

Page 70: *St. Juan Diego,* Miguel Cabrera, Wikimedia Commons, Public Domain

Page 70: *Jacinta and Francisco Marto,* Joshua Benoliel, Ilustração Portuguesa no. 610, 29 October 1917, Wikimedia Commons, Public Domain

Page 70: *Retrato de Hermano Miguel (Miguel Febres Cordero),* © Ministerio de Cultura y Patrimonio, photograph, 1900-1910

Page 71: *Don Bosco la Torino în 1880 (fotografie originală),* author unknown, Wikimedia Commons, Public Domain

Page 71: *Mother Frances Xavier Cabrini,* Photograph, Wikimedia Commons, Public Domain

Page 71: *Monseigneur Pacelli, représentant du pape à Berlin,* Agence Rol, Bibliothèque nationale de France, Wikimedia Commons, Public Domain

Page 71: St. Gregory the Great, Carlo Saraceni (1619), National Gallery, London

Page 77: *The Gleaners,* 1857, Jean-François Millet, Wikimedia Commons, Public Domain

Page 78: *Katharine Drexel,* © Br. Robert Lentz, OFM | www.trinitystores.com

Page 82: ©www.bradi-barth.org, Bradi-Barth

Page 83: *Bl. Pier Giorgio Frassati,* © Associazione Pier Giorgio Frassati - Rome

Page 83: *St. Francis,* Fransisco de Zurbaran (circa 1660), Wikimedia Commons, Public Domain

Page 83: *Bl. Jordan of Saxony, a fresco from a convent at Worms,* Wikimedia Commons, Public Domain

Page 83: *Gabriel of Our Lady of Sorrows,* photo Philippe Plet, 1899, Wikimedia Commons, Public Domain

Page 84: *Paulinus of Nola,* Linz Cathedral, Wikimedia Commons

Page 84: *St Nicholas of Bari,* Fra Angelico (circa 1395-1455), Wikimedia Commons, Public Domain

Page 84: *Santa Rosa de Lima,* Bartolomé Esteban Murillo (1617-1682), Wikimedia Commons, Public Domain

Page 84: *Vincent de Paul,* Simon François de Tours (1606-1671), Wikimedia Commons, Public Domain

Page 85: *Fabiola,* Jean-Jacques Henner (1829-1905), Wikimedia Commons, Public Domain

Page 85: *Saint Martin and the Beggar,* Unknown Master, Hungarian (active around 1490), Wikimedia Commons, Public Domain

Page 85: *St. Elizabeth of Hungary,* © Cecelia Lawrence

Page 85: *San Giuseppe Moscati,* Inviaggio, Wikimedia Commons

Page 86: *Bl. Solanus Casey,* © Sister Mariana. O.P., Dominican Sisters of Mary, Mother of the Eucharist

Page 86: *Portrait of Josephine Bakhita,* author unknown, Wikimedia Commons, Public Domain

Page 86: *Mary Magdalene,* Piero di Cosimo (1462-1522), Wikimedia Commons, Public Domain

Page 86: *Saint Augustine,* Philippe de Champagne (1602-1674)Wikimedia Commons, Public Domain

Page 87: *Depiction of Saint Ailred*, Alexander Penrose Forbes (1874), Wikimedia Commons, Public Domain

Page 87: *Saint Veronica with the Veil,* Mattia Preti (1665-1660), Wikimedia Commons, Public Domain

Page 87: *St. Martin de Porres,*© Sister Mariana, O.P., Dominican Sisters of Mary, Mother of the Eucharist

Page 87: *Saint Camillus de Lellis,* author unknown, Wikimedia Commons, Public Domain

Page 88: *Portrait of Bishop John Fisher,* Hans Holbein (1497/1498-1543), Wikimedia Commons, Public Domain

Page 88: *St. Polycarp* by Michael Burghers (c. 1685) http://guide.jamieoneill.com/i/03/0301_polycarp.jpg Wikimedia Commons, Public Domain

Page 88: *Sts. Basil and Gregory* by by Gerard Edelinck (c. 1707), Public Domain

Page 88: *Ignatius of Loyola* (engraving) by William Holl the Younger (1807-1871) - http://search2.famsf.org:8080/search.shtml?keywords=Younger&artist=&country=&period=&sort=&start=101, Public Domain, https://commons.wikimedia.org/w/index.php?curid=6080261

Page 89: *Claude de la Colombière,* author unknown Wikimedia Commons, Public Domain

Page 89: *St. Padre Pio,* © Julie Lonneman / www.trinitystores.com

Page 89: *Saint Catherine Labouré,* unidentfied photographer (1806-1876), Wikimedia Commons, Public Domain

Page 89: *St Matthew and the Angel,* Guido Reni (1575–1642), Wikimedia Commons, Public Domain

Page 90: *Louis IX ou Saint-Louis d'après le Recueil des rois de France de* Jean Du Tillet, 16th Century, Wikimedia Commons, Public Domain

Page 90: *The 'De Grey' Hours,* author unknown, 1390, Wikimedia Commons, Public Domain

Page 90: *Saint Patrick Catholic Church (Junction City, Ohio) - stained glass,* Saint Patrick, 2015, Wikimedia Commons, Creative Commons Attribution-Share Alike 3.0 Unported

Page 90: *St. Josaphat Saint of Ruthenia,* painting from an English church building, author unknown, Wikimedia Commons, Public Domain

Page 91: *St. Dominic,* Fra Angelico, 1441, Wikimedia Commons, Public Domain

Page 91: *St. Catherine of Siena,* © Cecilia Lawrence

Page 91: *Elisabeth of the Trinity* (face portrait), Willuconquer, Wikimedia Commons, Creative Commons Attribution-Share Alike 3.0 Unported

Page 91: *St. Hildegard of Bingen,* © Cecilia Lawrence

Page 92: *Bl. Anna Maria Taigi,* © Sr. Mary Ignatius, O.P., Dominican Sisters of Mary, Mother of the Eucharist

Page 92: *Father Damien,* (photo is from the Hawaii State Archives in Honolulu, Hawaii), 1889, Wikimedia Commons, Public Domain

Page 92: *Frances of Rome giving alms* (painting in Getty museum, Los Angeles), Giovanni Battista Gaulli (1639–1709), Wikimedia Commons, Public Domain

Page 92: *St Catherine of Alexandria* (painting), Raphael (1483–1520), Wikimedia Commons, Public Domain

Page 93: *Margaret of Scotland,* Hugo van der Goes (circa 1440–1482), Wikimedia Commons, Public Domain

Page 93: *St. Lawrence,* artist unknown, Marie-Lan Nguyen (User:Jastrow), 2008-12-26 (photographer), Wikimedia Commons, Public Domain

Page 93: *Portrait of Pius V, pope,* El Greco (1541–1614), 1600-1610, Wikimedia Commons, Public Domain

Page 93: *St Columba Altarpiece (detail),* Rogier van der Weyden, circa 1455, Wikimedia Commons, Public Domain

Page 94: *St. Peter Claver* (stained glass window in the Church of St. Mary Magdalene and St. Andrew in Dormagen in Rhein-Kreis Neuss (Nordrhein-Westfalen), photo by GFreihalter, Wikimedia Commons, Creative Commons Attribution 3.0 Unported

Page 94: *St Anthony of Padua with the Infant Christ*, Guercino, 1656, Wikimedia Commons, Public Domain

Page 94: *Polyptych of San Vincenzo Ferreri (central panel),* Giovanni Bellini, circa 1465, Wikimedia Commons, Public Domain

Page 94: *St Augustine of Canterbury (d.604) preaching before Ethelbert (552?-616) Anglo-Saxon king of Kent whom he baptised in 597. Augustine sent by Pope Gregory I to convert Anglo-Saxons to Christianity. First Archbishop of Canterbury.*

Colour-printed wood engraving, London, 1864 / Universal History Archive/UIG / Bridgeman Images
Page 95: *Blessed Anne Marie Javouhey*, © Sisters of St. Joseph of Cluny
Page 95: *The Martyrdom of Saint Tarcisius* by Antony Troncet, 1908, Wikimedia Commons, Public Domain
Page 95: *St. Bernard* by Georges Jansoone - Own work, Public Domain, https://commons.wikimedia.org/w/index.php?curid=910070
Page 95: *Agnes of Montepulciano* (Dominican-Order-church in Friesach: Main altar: Agnes of Montepulciano), by Neithan90 - Own work, CC0, https://commons.wikimedia.org/w/index.php?curid=12860141
Page 101: *Predella of the San Domenico Altarpiece (detail)*, Fra Angelico, National Gallery, Wikimedia Commons, Public Domain
Page 102: *Chiara Luce Badano*, used with permission by Catholicfundraisingideas.com
Page 103: U.S. Army Sgt. 1st Class Patrick Stoner and U.S. Army Sgt. Robert Huff rescue an Afghan man from encroaching flood waters in Nari Shahi village, Wikimedia Commons, Public Domain
Page 103: Army Maj. Ladda "Tammy" Duckworth of the Illinois Army National Guard's 1st Battalion, 106th Aviation Regiment, narrates the "Salute to Fallen Asian Pacific Islander Heroes," Wikimedia Commons, Public Domain
Page 105: *Finding in the Temple*, www.bradi-barth.org, Bradi-Barth
Page 106: *Saints Cyril and St. Methodius* by Walter from Tampa/St Petersburg, Florida - DSC_2139_pp, CC BY 2.0, https://commons.wikimedia.org/w/index.php?curid=64424038
Page 106: *St. Bede* by The original uploader was Timsj at English Wikipedia - Transferred from en.wikipedia to Commons., Public Domain, https://commons.wikimedia.org/w/index.php?curid=2259187
Page 106: *St. John Neumann* by By Unknown - Unknown, Public Domain, https://commons.wikimedia.org/w/index.php?curid=1226107
Page 106: *St. Anthony Mary Claret* by user Caracas1830 on en.wikipedia - http://www.oremosjuntos.com/SantoralLatino/SAntonioClaret3.jpg, Public Domain, https://commons.wikimedia.org/w/index.php?curid=1316887
Page 107: *St Filippo Neri in Ecstasy* by Guido Reni - Unknown, Public Domain, https://commons.wikimedia.org/w/index.php?curid=621224
Page 107: *St. Louis de Montfort*, by Auteur inconnu, mais l'image est très vieille et l'auteur est certainement mort depuis plus de 70 ans - Ancienne image religieuse, Public Domain, https://commons.wikimedia.org/w/index.php?curid=9951502
Page 107: *Martyrdom of Paul Miki* Credit: Wellcome Library, London. Wellcome Images images@wellcome.ac.uk http://wellcomeimages.org Martyrdom of Paul Miki S.J., Jacob Kisai S.J., John Goto S.J. and P. Petrus Battista in Japan in 1596. Engraving after A. van Diepenbeeck. Published: -
Page 107: *St. Turibius of Mongrovejo*, by User en:User:Polylerus on en.wikipedia - http://www.lepanto.com.br/Imagens/w0323.jpg The image was transferred from en.wiki (en:Image:Turibius.jpg) under the {{PD-old}} license tag. Wars, Public Domain, https://commons.wikimedia.org/w/index.php?curid=924144
Page 108: *St. Pope John Paul II* by uncredited; retouch of Image:JohannesPaulII.jpg - Public Papers of the Presidents of the United States - Photographic Portfolio--1993 Vol. II http://www.access.gpo.gov/nara/pubpaps/1993portv2.html, Public Domain, https://commons.wikimedia.org/w/index.php?curid=2089099
Page 108: *St. Maximilian Kolbe* by Joachim Schäfer - [1], Copyrighted free use, https://commons.wikimedia.org/w/index.php?curid=35220037
Page 108: St. Genevieve by Unknown, Public Domain, https://commons.wikimedia.org/w/index.php?curid=869298
Page 108: The martyrdom of St. Alban from a 13th Century manuscript of *The Life of St. Alban* by Matthew Paris was both scribe and illuminator for this manuscript., Public Domain, https://commons.wikimedia.org/w/index.php?curid=366070
Page 109: *St. Teresa of Calcutta*, by Noble36 - Own work, CC0, https://commons.wikimedia.org/w/index.php?curid=53876173
Page 109: St. Alphonsus Liguori: S. Alfonso Maria de Liguori - "Evangelizare Pauperibus Misit Me" by Giuseppe Antonio Lomuscio, 1988, licensed under Attribution-ShareAlike 4.0 International (CC BY-SA 4.0)- https://commons.wikimedia.org/wiki/File:S._Alfonso_Maria_de_Liguori_-_%22Evangelizare_Pauperibus_Misit_Me%22.jpg
Page 109: *St. Gianna Molla* © Sister Mariana, O.P., Dominican Sisters of Mary, Mother of the Eucharist.
Page 109: *St. Athanasius* by Dominichino (1609-1612), Public Domain.
Page 110: Servant of God Elisabeth Leseur: *Photo* (date unknown, died 1914), Public Domain.
Page 110: *St. Peter the Apostle* by Peter Paul Rubens (c. 1611), Public Domain
Page 110: *St. María Venegas de la Torre* © Sister Mariana, O.P., Dominican Sisters of Mary, Mother of the Eucharist
Page 110: St. Monica: St. Augustine and His Mother Monica by Ary Scheffer (1855), Public Domain
Page 117: *Lazarus in the House of the Rich Man*, 1610 (oil on panel), Francken, Hieronymus II (1578-1623) / Private Collection / Photo © Peter Nahum at The Leicester Galleries, London / Bridgeman Images
Page 118: *Venerable Matt Talbot*, © Sister Mary Ignatius, O.P., Dominican Sisters of Mary, Mother of the Eucharist
Page 122: ©www.bradi-barth.org, Bradi-Barth
Page 123: *St. Stephen from The Demidoff Altarpiece* by Carlo Crivelli (1476), Public Domain.
Page 123: *St. Bridget of Sweden* by Hermann Rode (late 15th century), Public Domain.
Page 123: *Bl. Henry Suso*. Anonymous (1601); Public Domain.
Page 123: *St. John Chrysosto Textlegende mit Datum 1601 m*, Hosios Loukas Monastery, (11th Century), Public Domain.
Page 124: St. Bernadette Soubirous, Photo (c. 1858), Public Domain
Page 124: *St. Bonaventure* by Claude Francios (c. 1655), Public Domain.
Page 124: *St. Joseph of Cupertino*, by Ludovico Mazzanti (17th Century), Public Domain.
Page 124: *St. Gemma Galgani, Photo* (date unknown) Public Domain.
Page 125: *Bl. Anthony Grassi*, Image date and artist unknown, (Source: Oxford Oratory, 2012)
Page 125: Ven. Pierre Toussaint: *Portrait of Venerable Pierre Toussaint,* Anonymous (1835); Public Domain.
Page 125: *St. John de Britto,* Anonymous (17th Century), Public Domain.
Page 125: *St. Thérèse of the Child Jesus, Photo* (April 14, 1894), Public Domain.
Page 126: *St. John XXIII, Photo, (*1959) Public Domain
Page 126: *St. John of God:* Passing of St. John of God, attributed to Juan Zapaca Inga (1684-1685), Public Domain.
Page 126: Bl. John Henry Newman, *Photo,* Public Domain.
Page 126: *St. Francis de Sales*, Anonymous, Public Domain.
Page 127: *St. Maria Goretti* by Giuseppe Brovelli-Soffredini (1929), Public Domain
Page 127: *St. Thomas Composing* by Dominican Sisters of Stone, Staffordshire (19th Century)
Page 127: *St. André Bessette: Photo* (1920), Public Domain
Page 127: *St. Bruno praying in the dessert* by Jean Restout (1763), Public Domain.
Page 128: *St. Benedict* by Fra Angelico (1437-1446), Public Domain.
Page 128: *Bl. Humbert of Romans,* Sister Mary Ignatius, OP, Dominican Sisters of Mary, Mother of the Eucharist
Page 128: *St. Raymond of Peñafort* by Tommaso Dolabella (1627), Public Domain.
Page 128: St. Albert the Great: detail from *The Cycle of Forty Illustrious Members of the Dominican Order* by Tommaso da Modena (1352), Public Domain.
Page 129: St. Perpetua: *Mary and Child with Saints Felicity and Perpetua (Sacra Conversazione)*, Anonymous (c. 1520).
Page 129: St. Anthony of Egypt
Page 129: Bl. Charles de Foucauld, *Photo* (c. 1916)
Page 129: *Portrait of St. Kateri Tekakwitha,* by Claude Chauchetière (c. 1690), Public Domain
Page 132: O*n the Road to Emmaus*, by Duccio, 1308-1311, Museo dell'Opera del Duomo, Siena. Wikimedia Commons, Public Domain.
Page 133: *Christ and the Rich Young Ruler* by Heinrich Hofmann (1889), Public Domain
Page 144: St. John Bosco*, Photo,* Public Domain.

ACKNOWLEDGEMENTS

In 2013, the first edition of the *Educator's Guide* came to fruition through the time and talents of many generous people. Their contributions still exist in this revised second edition, therefore I would like to extend my heartfelt gratitude to them: Fr. James Sullivan, OP, Fr. Thomas Petri, OP, Fr. Basil Cole, OP, Fr. David Meconi, SJ, and Dr. Mary Healy.

The Knights of Columbus granted permission to reprint excepts from Fr. Peter John Cameron, OP, *The Gift of the Holy Spirit*. Veritas Series. Connecticut: Knights of Columbus, 2002.

The illustrations in the virtue sections were drawn by students of *Spiritus Sanctus Academy* in Ann Arbor, Michigan. They were directed by the tireless (and yes, very patient) direction of Sr. Mary Grace Kamp, OP.

This second edition of *An Educator's Guide to Living a Virtuous Life* is the result of input offered by teachers, administrators, parents, and others desiring to restore a culture of virtue. I am tremendously grateful to Linda Kelly and Amy Beers for their tireless work in implementing numerous design and layout changes Additionally, I would like to thank Sally Wagner for always being willing to step in and assist us.

Finally, I want to express my gratitude to Mother Assumpta Long, OP, for supporting and encouraging us to develop the resources. Thank you to all the Sisters in my community, the Dominican Sisters of Mary, Mother of the Eucharist, for sharing this vision and striving to live it each day. In particular, I would like to thank Sister Jude Andrew Link, OP, for listening and speedily typing while I articulated the vision for the second edition. Her input and experience brought tremendous value to this revision. Sr. Emmanuel Gross, OP, lent her creative artistic talents in drawing the Kerygma tree. I would be remiss not to thank Sr. Maria Fatima Nunes, OP, and Sr. Maria Veritas Marks, OP, for their layout suggestions and to Sr. Joseph Andrew Bogdanowicz, OP, for meticulously reading every word. Finally, a big thank you to Sr. Mary Samuel Handwerker, OP, who enthusiastically shares the mission with those she meets.